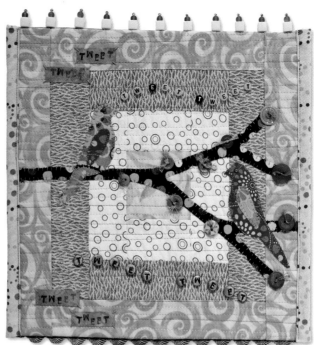

SEW
embellished!

artistic little quilts, personalized with easy techniques

Cheryl Lynch

Martingale®
Create with Confidence

ACKNOWLEDGMENTS

Creating can't be done in a vacuum. It requires ideas and inspiration to flow in many directions. Without my family, the quilting community, the many people who have come to hear my lectures and take my classes, and, of course, Martingale, this book would not be possible. Thank you to those I have met on my journey and to those of you I will meet in the future. I learn as much from you as you hopefully learn from me.

Sew Embellished! Artistic Little Quilts,
Personalized with Easy Techniques
© 2012 by Cheryl Lynch

Martingale®
19021 120th Ave. NE, Ste. 102
Bothell, WA 98011-9511 USA
ShopMartingale.com

Printed in China
17 16 15 14 13 12   8 7 6 5 4 3 2 1

**Library of Congress Cataloging-in-Publication Data
is available upon request.**

ISBN: 978-1-60468-147-5

Mission Statement

Dedicated to providing quality products and service to inspire creativity.

Credits

President & CEO: Tom Wierzbicki

Editor in Chief: Mary V. Green

Design Director: Paula Schlosser

Managing Editor: Karen Costello Soltys

Technical Editor: Nancy Mahoney

Copy Editor: Sheila Chapman Ryan

Production Manager: Regina Girard

Cover & Text Designer: Shelly Garrison

Illustrator: Laurel Strand

Photographer: Brent Kane

CONTENTS

INTRODUCTION

Accessories speak to me, whether the accessories are for personal adornment or to dress up my house or my table. I especially like items that have dangling beads or ribbons. I'm also smitten with the shape of shrines and with architectural details that add character to the rooflines of buildings. All of these details have inspired me to create embellished projects with unusual edges. The edge of a quilt is a perfect place to have fun with additional design details.

And how about if instead of working months and maybe a year on a quilting project, you could finish it in a day or two? I designed most of the projects in this book to be made in a short time. The length of time will be determined by whether you work solely with a sewing machine, solely by hand, or with a combination of both.

As a quilter, when you think of handwork, the most common technique that comes to mind is hand quilting. However, with the advent of machine quilting and especially free-motion quilting, I've found I can finish many more quilts if I use my machine for that part of the process. But with that said, I do love handwork. My hands always have to be busy, no matter what I'm doing. It relieves the guilt from sitting on my tush and also keeps the boredom away. Long car rides pass much faster when I have a project to work on. Waiting for my turn at a doctor's office can become enjoyable as I accomplish part of a project. I must confess that I love watching TV and if I'm creating something with my hands at the same time, I don't feel quite so decadent.

My love of beads and embroidery was the starting point for *Sew Embellished!* Both beading and embroidery are portable and can be done by hand. These are not new to the world of patchwork. Crazy quilts, incorporating beads and embroidery, reached their height of popularity in the late 19th century. But the stitching is very labor intensive and reminds me of the Victorian era. I was interested in something modern. I wanted to use modern techniques and modern materials.

I also wanted to use themes for my pieces. Themes of family, love, and life are integral to my projects. Themes also include family interests, such as sports and pets. You can incorporate your family's interests in your quilts, or include themes of current topics that impact our world, expressing them with fabric and embellishments.

So many components make up an embellished quilt. The choices you make for edge finishes, embellishments, and threadwork make each one unique. You can achieve a beautiful and meaningful piece in a reasonable amount of time, especially when the sewing machine is combined with handwork.

Use this book first as a primer for learning about different materials and techniques or adding to the ones you already know. Then use these techniques as you choose the different projects to create. But, tailor the project to *your* life, *your* family, and *your* interests. Make the projects your own. Remember, there's no limit to what can be put on a quilt that's going to be used as a piece of fiber art, as long as it's not going to be washed or used on a bed.

But most of all, have fun!

EMBELLISHING with beads, buttons, and other beautiful things

Adding embellishments to the surface of a quilt can bring beauty, glitz, design elements, color, texture, hardness or softness, as well as unexpected surprises. Bead, fabric, and craft stores are the most logical sources of embellishments, but I'm always on the hunt for unusual goodies. Alternative locations such as hardware stores, flea markets, and secondhand shops are good options. Online sources provide another good hunting ground.

BUTTONS

Many quilters have a fabric stash. I also have a button stash. They tend to accumulate, whether they're extra buttons that come with a new sweater, a button box inherited from a relative, or stray buttons found in the washing machine. One of my biggest regrets is that I didn't keep and cherish my mother's button tin. I didn't know how much I would come to love buttons at the time of her death and I don't even know what happened to them. But I'm definitely making up for that loss with my own collection.

Sort your buttons by color so the right button is easy to find when you need it.

I use buttons whether they have two holes or four. You can attach them by hand or machine, with the knot on the top or the bottom. Any type of thread can be used. If the buttons are attached individually, make a double knot and use a drop of seam sealant, such as Fray Check, on the knot to keep the button from coming loose.

Using different methods of attaching buttons adds interest to your project.

Buttons can also be added as a stacked group or attached with beads. They also look good clustered side by side. As with fabric, it's often interesting to use multiple types of buttons to achieve a scrappy look.

Pair buttons and beads to vary the texture of your embellishments.

A combination of a button, ribbon, and various sizes of beads makes a fun tassel.

Sewing buttons on by machine requires a sewing machine with a zigzag stitch. You must also be able to drop the feed dogs so that the fabric doesn't advance when stitching. Set the width of the zigzag stitch to match the distance between the buttonholes. Turn the flywheel by hand as you make any adjustments so that you don't inadvertently stitch into the button and break it or the needle.

I use an open-toe embroidery foot for stitching buttons so I can easily see the holes. Once everything is adjusted, stitch back and forth at least five times. If you're attaching buttons that are placed close together, don't cut the threads before moving on to the next button. Clip the threads after attaching the last button and add a drop of seam sealant.

BEADS, BEADS, BEADS

Thousands of different beads can be found in stores, catalogs, and websites that specialize in beads. You can even use inexpensive jewelry as a source for beads. Beads come in many different shapes, sizes, and colors. They can be made of glass, plastic, metal, and natural materials such as pearl, nut, seashell, ceramic, and minerals, among other substances. Most of them can be added to your quilt. Most beads are sized in millimeters (mm).

Mass-produced beads called seed beads are made of glass and are available in a large array of colors and standardized sizes. The most popular sizes range from small (11/0) to large (2/0). I find the 8/0 size to be the most versatile and useful.

For the projects in this book, you'll find size 8/0 beads (second from top) are the most useful.

protect your fabric

When choosing beads, it's important to note whether or not the bead would damage the fabric due to sharp points, oily content, bleeding from a dye, or rusting from a metal.

Long, thin glass beads, known as bugle beads, are available in varying lengths. Hexagons, triangular shapes, and even cubes are certain to add interest to a quilt. In addition to these very popular shapes, glass beads come in many other shapes and sizes. Choose beads that are an appropriate size and weight for your project.

It's important to use beading thread to attach beads. Beading thread is very strong and durable, so it's less likely to break than standard sewing thread. You'll find several different brands, all suitable. For more information, see "Threads" on page 12.

Choose a strong, thin needle to attach the beads, especially those with very small holes. Beading needles designed for creating jewelry are too long and thin, and bend too easily for attaching beads to fabric. The best needles for attaching beads are milliner's or straw needles. The needles range in size from 3 to 9; select a size that will easily fit through the hole in the bead. For more information, see "Needles" on page 14.

My definition of a bead is that it has one hole passing through it, as opposed to a button, which has two or four holes. With only one hole, a bead needs to be attached to the fabric differently than you would attach a button, where you go in one hole and out another. There are two basic ways to attach a single bead. In the first method, the bead is lying on its side with the hole in a horizontal position. In the second method, the bead is sitting with the hole facing vertically, top and bottom. To secure beads in a horizontal orientation, you only need to stitch through the bead once to secure it. If the bead is sitting vertically, and needs to stay that way, you'll need to bring the thread through the bead twice, on opposite sides, to keep it stable and upright.

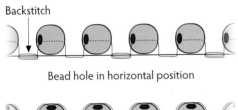

Bead hole in horizontal position

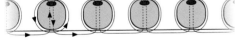

Bead hole in vertical position

I also like to use flat or disc-type beads. Flat beads look similar to buttons, but they only have one hole and are made of glass, metal, plastic, or plant material. Actually, anything flat and small with one hole can be an embellishment. Simply attach it with a seed bead or other small round bead.

Flat beads come in a variety of sizes, shapes, and materials.

embellishing tip

My best advice for beading is that the beads need to be very secure. They will never get tighter—but they can become loose. To prevent the thread from stretching *after* sewing, cut an 18" length and stretch it between your hands three or four times before sewing. Make sure the beads are stitched securely from the beginning. And when attaching multiple beads with one piece of thread, it's important to take small, invisible backstitches between every few beads. This will make sure that *all* the beads won't fall off even if one of them does.

IF IT HAS A HOLE, YOU CAN PUT IT ON YOUR QUILT

There are no rules for adding embellishments to your project as long as the quilt isn't meant to be used as a bed quilt or washed. If an object has a hole, it can be attached to fabric, as long as it's not too big or too heavy for the fabric to bear. Even if it doesn't have a hole, sometimes you can make a hole or figure out another way to attach the item.

When I roam the aisles of hardware stores, my best finds are usually washers. Washers come in lots of different sizes. Usually they're the silver color of stainless steel, but you can also find brass washers as well as black or red rubber washers. Lock washers look like little gears.

Imagine the fun details you can create with these assorted inexpensive washers from the hardware store!

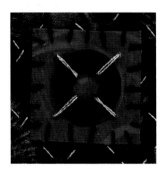

Use a whipstitch to attach washers to your projects.

As well as being used to attach flat beads, seed beads can be used for securing other types of similar embellishments, such as sequins, charms, and buttons. Sequins can add color and a bit of sparkle to a project, and often make the fabric look like it has polka dots on it. Whenever an embellishment has one hole, use a stop bead to attach it to the surface of the quilt. It's called a stop bead because the bead stops the thread from slipping through the single hole in other embellishments.

Sequins come in many different sizes, shapes, and colors.

Three seed beads strung together make a charming center for a flower sequin.

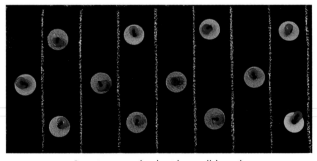

Sequins attached with small beads or seed beads add visual texture.

Look for other novelty items to attach to your project. Some items, such as charms, are meant for crafting, but other doodads—like old keys, Chinese coins, and snaps—all had other original uses. Don't let that stop you from using them on a little quilt!

Spice up a project with any of these novelties used as embellishments.

Detail of rickrack and beads used in "Family Musings in Blue" (see page 76 for the full project).

TRIMS WITH BEADS

Trims are not just suitable for the top and bottom edges of a project. Trims, such as ribbon, lace, and rickrack, can be used in many areas on the surface of the quilt. They can be used alone or embellished with sequins, beads, and French knots.

Detail of trim, sequins, and seed beads used in "From the Bottom of My Heart" (see page 64 for the full project).

Trims come in so many colors, styles, widths, and materials that you're sure to find one—new or vintage—to suit your project.

POLYMER-CLAY embellishments

I discovered polymer clay when I couldn't find the right embellishment for a project. I could visualize what I wanted and looked all over for it. As a solution I decided to make it myself. I hung out in the pottery studio when I was a graduate student at MIT, so how hard could it be? As it turned out, it wasn't hard at all.

POLYMER-CLAY BASICS

You'll need to know a few basics before creating clay embellishments. First of all, polymer clay is not truly clay—it's really a plastic. It comes in many different colors and can be found at your local craft store. Unlike clay, you don't need a kiln to harden polymer buttons or beads. Baking polymer-clay objects in a low-temperature oven makes them durable. A wonderful attribute of polymer clay is that it never gets hard without being baked. I mean *never*. I've had some in a drawer, unwrapped for two years, and it's still soft and pliable.

Polymer clay can be used to make buttons and beads in many different colors. When you open the package, the clay is very stiff and needs to be conditioned. To warm and condition the clay, knead it with your hands for three to five minutes until it can be shaped into a soft ball. Sometimes, I put it in my pocket and let it warm up for 10 to 15 minutes. The three most readily available polymer clays are Sculpey III, Premo Sculpey, and Fimo. Sculpey III is the easiest one to use.

Create beads and buttons using polymer clay, plastic coffee stirrers, and saftey-razor blades.

In addition to the polymer clay, to create beads and buttons you'll need parchment paper, plastic coffee stirrers for making uniform holes in the clay, clear acrylic sealer, single-edge safety-razor blades for cutting the clay, gold spray paint, and wet wipes.

BASIC BUTTONS

The easiest buttons start with a ball of clay that you flatten. Start with a ½"-diameter ball. I like to work on a sheet of parchment paper, and I keep wet wipes nearby to clean my hands. The best way to form a clean hole in your clay button is to use a coffee stirrer. Poke it straight through the button with a little twist of the wrist. The smaller the hole, the better. Just make sure the hole is the same size as or larger than your sewing needle. The best way to create the size of button you want is through trial and error.

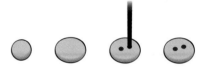

IMPRESSION BUTTONS

You can make a more intricate button simply by making an impression in the clay with a commercial button. To easily remove the commercial button from the clay button you're making, insert string through the buttonholes and secure with a knot. Press the button into a ball of the clay, and then remove the button by carefully pulling on the string.

The options are limited only by the buttons you use to create an impression.

Any item with texture can be used to make an impression in the clay. You can use a doily, plant material, or a rubber stamp. The only limit is your imagination. To make the impression stand out, paint or stain it after baking.

A rubber stamp, a bit of cedar, or even a piece of lace can be used to make an impression in a polymer-clay button.

CONSISTENT SIZING

Sometimes the biggest challenge is making uniform-sized beads or buttons. The best way to achieve uniform beads is to start with an equal amount of clay for each. When trying to create relatively uniform embellishments, I always make more than I need, and then choose the ones that are most alike. They will never be identical.

1. Lay a piece of parchment paper on a cutting mat. Roll the conditioned clay into a snake, like you did when you were a kid; a ½"-wide snake works well for buttons.

2. Using a single-edge safety-razor blade, cut slices of equal thickness.

3. Roll each slice into a ball. Flatten with your thumb to create buttons or leave it round to make a bead. To make holes for sewing, poke a coffee stirrer through the center of the clay. You can make one or two holes.

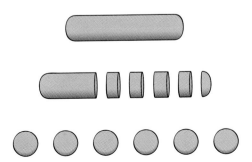

POLKA-DOT BUTTONS

Another fun technique is to add polka dots to the buttons. Follow steps 1 and 2 in "Consistent Sizing" at left to make two different-colored snakes. Make a ½"-wide snake for the buttons and a 1/16"-wide snake for the polka dots.

Partially flatten the larger balls. Then place three or four smaller balls on top of the flattened clay. Cover with a small piece of parchment paper. Using a ruler, flatten the pieces evenly to create polka-dot buttons. Then use a coffee stirrer to make holes for attaching the buttons.

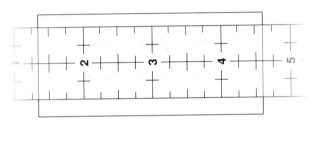

BEADS

You can make beads in a similar manner to making buttons. The difference is that you make only one hole and you don't flatten the clay as much. When making multiple beads, I use a 12-gauge wire to create the holes and leave the beads on the wire for baking.

BAKING AND FINISHING

As a health precaution, don't use the same utensils you used to create clay buttons and beads when cooking food. I bake my embellishments on a piece of parchment paper placed on a cookie sheet in a toaster oven. Follow the directions on the package for baking the clay. *Do not* cook food at the same time you're baking the beads or buttons. If you're going to be doing a lot of polymer-clay work, it's best to have a dedicated toaster oven used strictly for crafting. Good ventilation, such as a kitchen fan, is important if you're making a lot of beads or buttons.

To achieve a metallic look, spray the beads or buttons with a metallic paint after baking and cooling. Then seal them with a clear acrylic spray. To highlight an impression in the clay, such as a plant, paint the clay with a water-soluble acrylic paint. Before the paint has a chance to dry, carefully wipe the paint off with a soft cloth. The paint will remain in the impression.

Make a personalized plaque
using a rubber stamp and gold paint.

THREAD as a design element

I never met a thread for hand sewing that I didn't like. Some threads are the stars of a particular design, while others play a supporting role. The secret to using any thread is to choose the appropriate needle. This applies to both machine and hand stitching. The key to success is a sharp needle with an eye that's not too large, yet large enough to accommodate the thread.

THREADS

Threads come in a variety of fiber contents, plies, and thicknesses. Each thickness is given a number designation; larger numbers indicate thicker thread. There's a limit to the thickness of thread you can use, based on what will fit through the weave of the fabric. If a thread starts to fray or tangle, use a shorter length. A thread conditioner, such as Thread Heaven or beeswax, will sometimes help keep threads from tangling.

Threads are available as pure fibers and also as mixed-fiber contents. Each provides a different look to a project. As long as you're embellishing a wall hanging, there are no rules about which threads to use with which type of fabric. If you like it, use it. Even if a thread is made for machine use, there's no reason you can't also use it for hand stitching. I've had success with threads made of cotton, rayon, wool, polyester, and metallic materials.

The most commonly available threads for hand sewing are six-ply embroidery floss and pearl cotton. Pearl cotton is available in a variety of thicknesses. Pearl cotton and embroidery floss come in a myriad of colors and are readily available at all of the chain craft stores.

Embroidery floss and pearl cotton

Rayon is a wonderful thread to use for its sheen and luster. It's available as stranded floss that can be separated for hand sewing and as spooled thread designed for machine use.

Various types of rayon threads

Wool thread can be 100% wool fibers or blended with acrylic, to add strength. Blended wool thread can be stitched with a sewing machine and isn't only for using with wool fabric. Wool thread is somewhat "hairy" and gives stitches a nice texture on any fabric.

Different brands of wool thread

The type of polyester thread I prefer is usually made for machine work and is widely available at chain sewing stores. When using it for hand stitching, I use at least two strands held together with a knot at one end.

Polyester thread comes in a variety of colors.

Metallic thread comes mixed with many different fibers and in many different thicknesses. It's a wonderful thread to use as both the "star" of a piece and as a supporting thread. It can add just the right touch of bling.

Metallic threads range from subtle glitz to shimmering.

One other essential thread for embellishing is nylon beading thread. Look for either Nymo or Silamide brand. They both come in an assortment of colors and are fine yet very strong. Only a few colors are necessary to blend with different bead colors, such as light, dark, and medium gray.

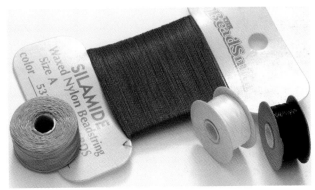
Nylon beading thread

NEEDLES

It's essential to have an assortment of embroidery, chenille, and milliner's needles to suit all the different thicknesses of threads you'll be using for embellishing and beading. These are all sharp needles, designed to pierce the threads of most fabrics. Whatever the type of needle, the smaller the number, the larger the needle.

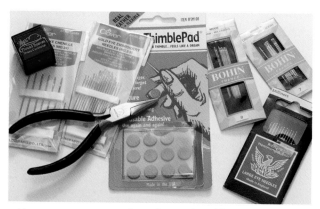

Have an assortment of needles on hand for embellishing. Finger protection, such as a ThimblePad, will shield your skin, and small pliers will help pull the needle and thick threads through the fabric.

When choosing a needle, you'll want to achieve a balance between the ease of threading the needle and the size of the hole it will make in the fabric. The goal is to use the needle with the smallest eye that can be threaded easily. If the eye is too small, the thread may fray. If the needle is too big, it will leave a hole in the fabric.

There are two instances in particular where the needle choice is essential. The first is when working a French knot. To achieve a nice tight knot that easily slides off the needle, use an embroidery needle with a slim eye profile.

The second instance is for beading. Traditional beading needles are too flimsy for adding beads as embellishments. Milliner's needles, also known as straw needles, have a round eye and an even-diameter shaft, making them easy to thread and a perfect size for fitting through 11/0 seed beads. Also, they won't bend as easily while traveling through fabric.

A small pair of pliers can help pull a needle through fabric in difficult situations. Finger protection, such as a soft thimble or thimble pad, will keep your fingers from being pricked.

ALL THE STITCHES YOU'LL NEED

Using hand-embroidery stitches can add beauty, interest, and design elements to your projects. The stitches I use are all basic stitches and are pretty easy to master. You can pair any thread choice with any stitch for wonderful results. To vary the effects, try different thicknesses of thread, or use more or fewer strands of floss.

Running stitch. This is the simplest stitch of all. The goal is to have the stitch the same length as the space between stitches. Bring the needle up at A and down at B. Repeat, bringing the needle up at A and down at B. Continue in the same manner.

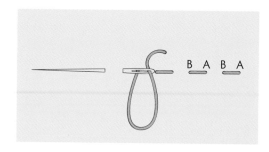

Big stitch. This stitch, also used for utility quilting, is similar to the running stitch, but the stitches are longer—and so are the spaces between them. It's traditionally done after the project is layered with backing and batting.

Backstitch. This is the best stitch for a continuous line and is perfect for stitching words on fabric. The stitches should be of equal size; if it's a curvy design, use smaller stitches for a smoother look. Bring the needle up at A and down at B. Repeat, bringing the needle up at C and down at A. Continue in the same manner.

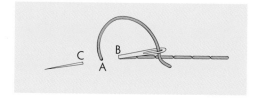

Blanket stitch. This is the traditional stitch used along the edges of fusible-appliqué motifs. Starting at the edge of the appliqué, bring the needle up at A. Insert the needle at B and reemerge at C, keeping the thread underneath the needle when it emerges at C. Pull the thread through to form a loop that lies under the emerging thread. The loop should lie snugly against the fabric without pulling or distorting it.

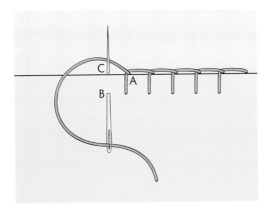

Whipstitch. I often use this modern version for stitching around fusible-appliqué motifs. It's less bulky and lends itself to unusual threads. It's also useful for attaching embellishments such as washers and foam letters. Bring the needle up at A and down at B. Repeat, bringing the needle up at A and down at B. Continue in the same manner.

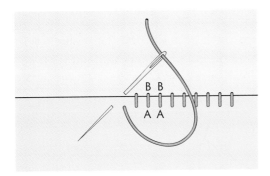

Chicken scratch. This is a fun and random stitch used to fill in a background. The stitches should be of equal length and stitched at varying angles. Bring the needle

up at A and down at B. Reemerge at C and continue in the same manner.

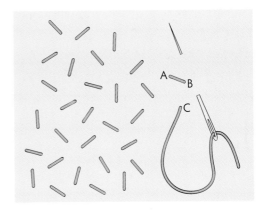

Cross-stitch. Bring the needle up at A and down at B. Reemerge at C and bring the needle back down at D. Continue in the same manner.

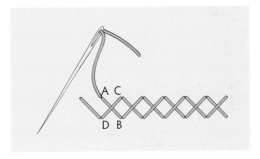

French knot. This stitch should result in a nice tight knot that sits right on top of the fabric surface. Using an embroidery needle, bring the needle up at A. Holding the thread with the left hand, wrap the thread around your needle two or three times. (The number of wraps determines the size of the knot.) Reinsert the needle at B, right next to A. Hold the thread taut so that it doesn't tangle as you pull the thread through to the back of your work.

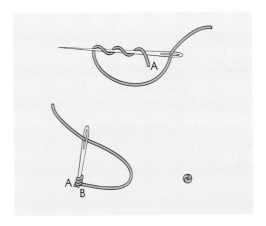

There are many times when I want to put words on my quilts, whether it's to include someone's name, express a sentiment, or even include a date. There are limited means to achieve this with traditional methods of quilting. So I developed a toolbox of other techniques.

Putting words on fabric is a very simple process. One of the most important considerations is to make sure if you're using ink—from a pen, marker, or laser printer—that it's colorfast and won't damage your quilt. Even though you may not plan on washing the quilt, you never know when it may get splashed with water or placed on a wet countertop. Even getting caught in the rain could ruin all of your work.

WRITING WITH PENS AND MARKERS

The easiest and simplest way to put words on fabric is with pens, markers, or paint pens. To start, you'll need to stabilize the fabric so it doesn't shift while you're writing. You can use freezer paper for a removable stabilizer, or paper-backed fusible web if you want to fuse the words in place later.

Freezer paper can be found in most supermarkets. It has a shiny, plastic side and a paper side. Press the shiny side to the wrong side of the fabric using an iron set to the hottest temperature recommended for the fabric and *no* steam. Press on both the fabric side and the paper side for a very strong bond. After writing on the fabric, peel off the freezer paper.

Choosing an appropriate pen or marker that will not wash out or run requires testing. Some markers are labeled "permanent," but the drawn line may not stay crisp. Sometimes the ink bleeds. It's also important to determine the right thickness of the line. Also note that inks may behave differently on different fabrics. On one fabric a marker may give a nice crisp line, while the same marker may bleed on another fabric. Experiment and always test first.

Notice how the same pen writes clearly on one fabric and bleeds on the other. Be sure to test your pen on the fabric you'll use in the project before committing to it!

Determine how well you want to see the writing. Sometimes you may want it to be clear and very easy to read. Other times you may want it to be more of a hidden message. Also don't limit yourself to black ink. There are a wide variety of colors and metallic writing tools that will give wonderful results.

Control how much of a statement your message makes by using a busy or plain fabric.

STITCHING WORDS WITH THREAD

This technique has been used for hundreds of years. Any style of writing and any type of thread can be used. The stitching can be done without a pattern, or you can use a water-soluble marker as a guide. Refer to "All the Stitches You'll Need" on page 14 for instruction on making various stitches.

PRINTING DIGITALLY

The word-processing program on your computer is a very handy tool for putting your thoughts and words on fabric. You have a choice of many fonts to suit the theme or mood of the piece. Not only can you change the size of the font, you can also opt for a different color. Digital printing is a great design tool. (If you're not familiar with the word-processing program on your computer, refer to the owner's manual or the program's Help feature on how to use the fonts.)

When printing digitally, it's important that the ink is permanent. There are a few options to make this happen. First, commercially pretreated fabric sheets can be used with any printer, resulting in printing that won't wash out or run. The quality of these sheets varies, and a little experimentation will help you choose the ones you like the best. Be sure that the package says "colorfast." Follow the directions on the package.

Many quilters use their computer printers to make quilt labels, but why not use yours to add information to the front of your quilt using pretreated fabric sheets?

The other option is to print on non-treated fabric. To feed the fabric through your printer, you'll need to stiffen or stabilize it. The best method is to iron the shiny side of freezer paper to the wrong side of the fabric. To get a good seal, cut 9" x 12" pieces of the fabric *and* freezer paper. After ironing with a hot, dry iron, trim the stabilized fabric to 8½" x 11". If the fabric doesn't feed through smoothly, set the printer, or printing options, to the envelope setting.

The problem is that many inkjet-printer inks are not permanent. They may fade with washing or disappear completely. However, some Epson printers use a permanent, archival ink called DuraBrite that is pigment based. Pigment-based inks are colorfast,

which means that printing on any fabric will result in a colorfast print. There are a few other inkjet printers that use pigment-based ink as well.

Words can be printed on different types and colors of fabric.

APPLIQUÉING LETTERS

You can also use a word-processing program on your computer to create appliqué templates. Choose a font and a size that works for your particular project. When picking a font, try to avoid letters with very thin sections. Applying bold formatting to the font can sometimes help make letters more usable.

To prepare letters for fusible appliqué, use a pencil to trace the letters in *reverse* onto the paper side of the fusible web. If needed, use a light source, such as a light box or window, to clearly see the lines for tracing. The letters in this book have been drawn in reverse for fusible appliqué. Following the manufacturer's instructions, use an iron to press the fusible web with traced image onto the wrong side of the fabric. Use sharp scissors to cut out the letters, cutting directly on the traced lines. Remove the paper backing. Position and fuse the appliqués in place.

Stitch the letters in place by hand or machine. By hand, use a whipstitch, running stitch, blanket stitch, or French knots around the edges of each letter. Refer to "All the Stitches You'll Need" on page 14 for detailed instructions as needed. For machine stitching, you can use a blanket stitch, zigzag stitch, or straight stitch to secure the letters in place.

STAMPING WORDS WITH INK

Stamping on fabric using ink and rubber stamps offers many possibilities. You'll find alphabets in many sizes and fonts. You can mix and match them. The key to this technique is making sure that the ink on the stamp pad is permanent. Look for dye-based ink, and always test for colorfastness before preparing the final piece.

Alphabet rubber stamps come in a variety of sizes and fonts.

STAMPING WORDS WITH POLYMER CLAY

Another fun way to make a dimensional message is to use rubber stamps with polymer clay. You can impress words, dates, initials, or whatever you wish into individual beads or little plaques. Refer to "Polymer-Clay Embellishments" on page 10 for detailed instructions for working with polymer clay.

Poking a hole in each corner of your stamped polymer-clay plaque makes it easy to attach to fabric with floss or thread.

ATTACHING READY-MADE LETTERS

Foam letters are located in the children's section of large craft stores. They come in various sizes, colors, and font styles. If you can't find the right color in the size you want, spray paint them!

These letters have adhesive on the back. Simply peel off the protective paper layer and stick the letters on the fabric. Then whipstitch the letters in place to secure them. You can use any type of thread.

Foam letters add fun to little quilts.

Occasionally you'll come across charms or beads that can also be used to form words. Attach them as you would any other beads or charms.

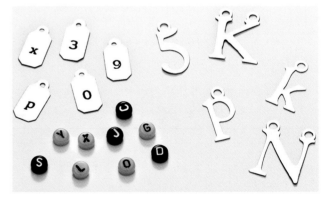

Metal charms and plastic or ceramic beads add a dimensional message to your project.

The top and bottom edges of a quilt are often forgotten, but they too can be embellished. Adding embellishments to these edges gives the piece a very ethnic feel. Morocco, anyone?

Finishing the top and bottom edges involves turning the project inside out; therefore some of the embellishments along these edges must be stitched between the front and back layers before turning. For more information about finishing, see "Assembling Your Project" on page 24.

CROWNS

Fabric triangles, used to finish the edges on a project, are often called *prairie points*. When I use them to adorn the top edge of an embellished project, I call them *crowns*. Crowns can be all one size or they can be assorted sizes.

1. You'll always start with a square. Press the square in half, wrong sides together.

2. Fold one corner toward the center on the diagonal and align the raw edges. Press.

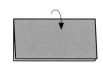

3. Repeat step 2, folding the other corner toward the center and press.

4. When the project is completely finished, the side with the folded edges should face the back of the project. With that in mind, position the crowns along the top edge with the folded side facing up as shown. Baste 1/8" from the raw edge to hold the crowns in place.

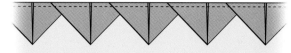

JEWELS

When a folded triangle is used along the bottom of a project, I called it a *jewel*. A jewel is constructed and positioned in the same manner as a crown. You can use a fabric square or you can make an elongated jewel using a rectangle.

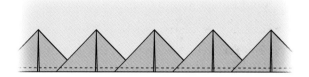

1. To make an elongated jewel, start with a 4½" x 6" rectangle of fabric. Along the bottom edge, fold over ½" to the wrong side of the fabric and press.

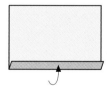

2. With the wrong side facing up, fold one corner diagonally toward the center. Press.

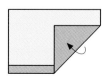

3. Fold the other corner diagonally toward the center as shown and press. Envision the jewel divided into parts marked A, B, and C.

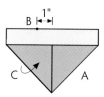

4. Fold the jewel, aligning the A folded edge with B. Press.

5. Fold the other side so that the C folded edge lines up with the folded edge on the opposite side. Press; turn the jewel over and trim off the excess fabric.

6. Position the jewels along the bottom edge with the folded side facing up as shown. Baste ⅛" from the raw edge to hold the jewels in place.

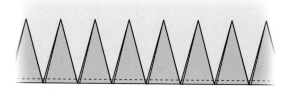

RICKRACK

Rickrack is another fun way to draw attention to the top and bottom edges of your project. The best width to use for small projects is ½" or ⅝" wide. Align the edge of the rickrack with the top or bottom edge on the front of the project. Baste ⅛" from the raw edge to hold the rickrack in place. The edges will be sewn into the seam allowance during the finishing stage.

For more embellishing, after binding the side edges, add sequins and/or beads to the rickrack. You can add lace trim in the same manner as rickrack.

BEADED TRIM

Purchased trim adds an exciting element to your project. However, this embellishment is only suitable for the bottom edge because of its fringe-like properties. With this type of beading, the beads are attached to the edge of a ribbon and the ribbon is hidden in the seam. Measure the width of the ribbon to determine the width of your seam allowance. If the ribbon is ¼" wide, align the edge of the ribbon with the right side facing down and the trimmed, raw edge on the front of the project. Baste ⅛" from the edge. When finishing the project, use a ¼"-wide seam allowance and a zipper foot to prevent getting stuck on the beads. If the ribbon is wider than ¼", adjust the width of the seam allowance accordingly.

BEADED EDGES

Add some sparkle and dimension to the top and bottom edges of your project with beads. This embellishing needs to be done after the top/bottom edges are finished and preferably after the binding is attached to the side edges. Decide how many beads are to be attached and place little tick marks for placement. Use a stop bead to secure a length of beads. With a milliner's needle and beading thread, sew on the beads. After going through the last bead, insert the needle through a stop bead, and then back through the preceding beads. After each addition of hanging beads, take a small, hidden backstitch for security.

Use beading to enhance rickrack and jewels along the bottom edge of your project.

Beads along the top edge need to stand up; consequently there's a limit to the size and number of beads.

Along the bottom edge, any size and number of beads can be used.

RIBBON AND DECORATIVE THREADS

After your piece is finished and bound, it's still not too late to add a bit of bling using ribbons and decorative threads. Use a sharp needle with a big eye and sew through the bottom edge; a small pair of pliers may be needed to pull the needle and ribbon through the fabric. Tie off the ribbon, trim the ends, and embellish with beads, if desired.

Ribbon and beads add glitz to the bottom edge.

FABRIC options

When it comes to selecting fabric for an embellished project, there are five factors to consider:

- How much embellishing do you plan on doing?
- What size is your project?
- Does your project have a focus?
- Are you planning to add appliqué?
- Are you willing to use fabrics with a fiber content that's not 100% cotton?

HOW MUCH EMBELLISHING?

The first decision to make before choosing fabrics for your project is how much embellishing you plan to do. If you're going to spend the time stitching and beading your fabric, you want your hard work to be seen. Embellishments and hand stitching will be lost on a busy background fabric.

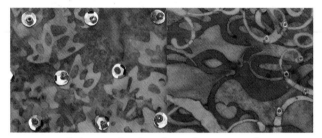

Fabrics with a lot of visual texture tend to overpower any embellishments.

Beads, buttons, and stitching will be more noticeable on a solid fabric, a tone-on-tone fabric, or fabric with a small print. Other fabric options are prints with open areas between motifs or prints with dots, crisscrossed lines, or stripes. These types of fabrics can be enhanced with beads, sequins, and/or buttons.

Embellishing creates a pattern on a solid fabric.

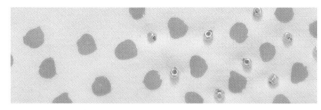

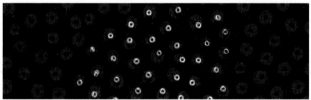

Adding embellishments to printed fabric creates a new design.

SIZE OF PROJECT

The size of your project is also important when choosing fabrics. Smaller-scale prints should be used for the small projects in this book. Large-scale prints are too busy. They will overwhelm a small project and interfere with the overall design. Make sure all the fabrics play well together in small pieces.

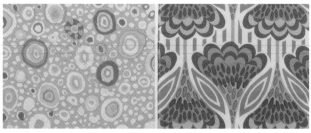

The scale in the pink-dot fabric is appropriate for small projects. The large-scale flowers in the other fabric will overpower the design.

PROJECT FOCUS

If your project has a special focus, such as a photo, appliqué, or embroidery, your fabrics need to be supporting players. You want to keep the spotlight on the focus part of the piece and not detract from it. Choose fabrics that are complementary and don't scream "look at me!" Balance is critical.

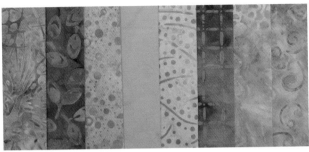

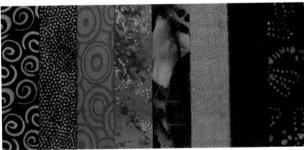

Examples of good fabric combinations

ADDING APPLIQUÉ

The weave of the fabric becomes important if your design includes appliqué, whether it's fusible or with a turned-under edge. A fabric with a tighter weave is preferable for appliqué. A loosely woven fabric will tend to ravel. This issue will really become problematic with curved designs. Pull the threads on a cut edge of the fabric, even while it's still on the bolt in the store. If you can see the threads start to separate, don't choose this fabric for appliqué. However, if you end up with a fabric that you just have to use and it frays, spray the fabric with starch and press before cutting out the appliqués to minimize fraying.

FIBER CONTENT

Most quilters prefer 100% cotton fabric. It's readily available in a wide range of colors and patterns, and is easy to work with. However, I love all kinds of fabric. The fiber content is not always important to me. Silk, organza, lamé, satin, and even polyester can add elegance and a bit of glitz to a project. They look like solids, but add texture and interest. Some of these fabrics will fray just by looking at them! Add fusible web or lightweight stabilizer on the wrong side to tame them. A word of caution: Be very careful with your iron. Turn down the temperature and always test the setting on a scrap of the fabric. Also, most of these fabrics require that you use a sharp pair of scissors and sharp needles whether you're working by hand or machine.

Step up the drama with various types of fabrics.

Heavyweight interfacing and varied edge treatments will make your project unique and will ensure that no one mistakes it for a pot holder!

Below is a list of the supplies you're likely to need, followed by step-by-step instructions for my basic construction methods.

USEFUL SUPPLIES

The items in this list are used in many of the projects and can be universally applicable. If you don't already have them on hand, you'll want to gather them before starting your project.

Double-sided heavyweight fusible interfacing. This interfacing is used in almost all of the projects. It has a heat-activated fusible web on both sides and makes the project very stiff. You can sew through it. A widely available brand is Peltex II. (The II means fusible on both sides.) Always follow the manufacturer's instructions for the product you are using.

Batting. Low-loft batting is used for all of the projects in the book. The fiber content doesn't matter. These small projects are a good place to use any batting scraps that you have on hand.

Fray Check. This liquid seam sealant comes in a small bottle. It's the best product for keeping threads from fraying and it dries clear.

Fabric-marking tools. The color of the fabric marker you choose is determined by the color of the fabric that needs to be marked. Sometimes a temporary marking tool, like chalk, will do the job; other times a little more long-lasting mark is needed. Blue water-soluble markers have the most versatility. Use white marking pencils to mark dark fabric. When using water-soluble markers and pencils, always follow the manufacturer's directions to remove the marks.

Spray box. A spray box is a very useful tool for catching overspray whether you're spraying with temporary adhesive or spray paint. It's crucial to keep the spray contained. A cardboard box is inexpensive and convenient. Test the box to make sure it's large

enough to protect from any overspray. When you spray, make sure it's in a well-ventilated area.

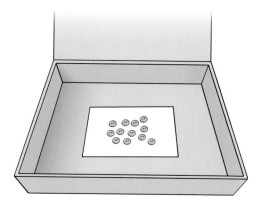

ASSEMBLING YOUR PROJECT

1. After the front of the piece is finished, trim and square up the top and bottom edges, trimming away the excess batting. You can trim the piece to the given dimensions or trim it to make the most of your piece. After trimming, locate and mark the center of the top and bottom edges with a pin.

2. Choose and prepare embellishments for the top and bottom edges as desired. Center the embellishments on the right side of the piece with the raw edges aligned. (The embellishment should

be positioned upside down relative to its final position.) Pin and machine baste in place, ⅛" from the edge. Remove the centering pins.

3. Measure the distance between the top and bottom edges. Cut the backing fabric to the same measurement. Center the backing on top of the front, right sides together. Sew the pieces together along the top and bottom edges using a ¼"-wide seam allowance.

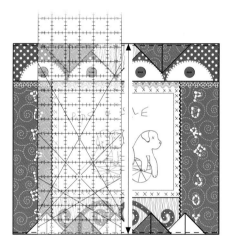

4. Measure the distance between the top and bottom stitching lines. Cut the interfacing to fit that measurement. The interfacing should be about 1" wider than the piece.

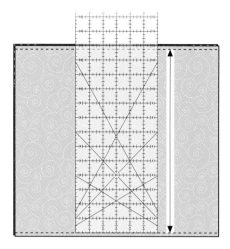

5. Turn the piece right side out and insert the interfacing between the front and back layers. It will seem tight, but adjust and smooth the fabric until the interfacing fits between the top and bottom seams. (There will be excess interfacing sticking out the sides.)

Interfacing

6. To protect the embellishments, use a hand towel for padding. Place the project, right side down, on top of the hand towel and press with a hot,

dry iron. The project should lie flat and the layers should be fused together.

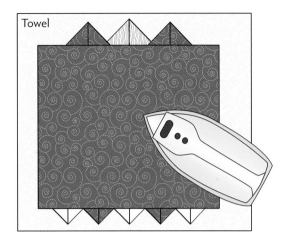

Towel

7. Trim each side, placing the ruler on the outside of the project to avoid the embellishments. Using the lines on a cutting mat as a guide and the given dimensions for trimming, trim the excess fabric and interfacing, being sure to cut through all the layers. If you're right-handed, trim the left side of the piece first, and then rotate it 180° to trim the other side. Reverse this procedure if you're left-handed. Now you're ready for binding.

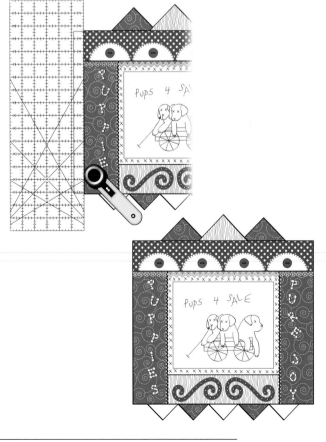

BINDING OPTIONS

Only the side edges need binding since the top and bottom edges are already finished. Try each of these three methods. All of them are done by machine.

Double-Fold Binding

This method is similar to the double-fold binding used on most quilts.

1. Start with two 2½"-wide strips of binding fabric that equal the length of the project plus 1". For example, if the length of the project is 9", the binding strips should measure 2½" x 10". Fold each strip in half lengthwise, wrong sides together, and press.

2. With the back of the project facing up, align the long raw edge of the binding strip with the raw edge on one side of the project, leaving a ½" tail at the top. Wrap this tail around the top edge to the front of the project.

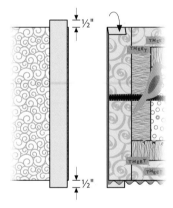

3. Starting with a backstitch, sew the binding to the project using a ¼"-wide seam allowance and a walking foot. Stop 2" from the bottom edge with the needle in the down position. Fold the ending tail of the binding snugly around the bottom of the project to the front. Finish stitching, ending with a backstitch.

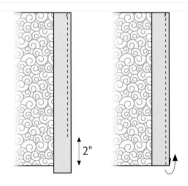

4. Fold the binding to the front. Pin the binding in place, covering the line of machine stitches and tucking in the ends. To finish, sew a straight line of stitches close to the folded edge or use a machine blanket stitch.

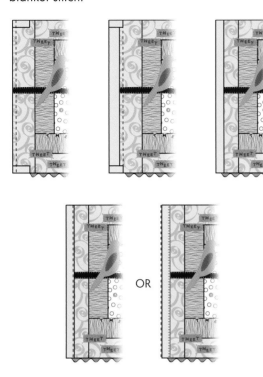

Fusible Binding

1. Apply fusible web to the wrong side of the binding fabric. Cut two 1"-wide strips of binding fabric that equal the length of the project plus 1". (For example, if the length of the project is 9", the binding strips should measure 1" x 10".) *Do not* remove the paper backing yet. Optionally, use a rotary cutter with a pinking blade to cut the strips. Fold each strip in half lengthwise, wrong sides together, and press. After the binding strips have cooled, remove the paper backing.

2. Lay the project face up on a piece of parchment paper so the binding doesn't accidentally fuse to the ironing board. With ½" of the binding extending beyond the top edge, align the crease in the binding with the edge of the project. Press the binding in place, being careful not to damage any of the embellishments.

3. Fold the binding to the back and press. Trim the excess binding from the top and bottom edges.

4. Stitch along the raw edge as shown.

Button Binding

1. Start with two 2½"-wide strips of binding fabric that equal the length of the project plus 1". (For example, if the length of the project is 9", the binding strips should measure 2½" x 10".) On each short end, fold over ½" to the wrong side and press. Press the strip in half lengthwise, wrong sides together. Repeat with the second strip.

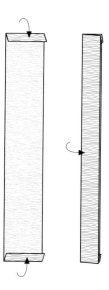

2. Open each binding strip and fold both raw edges to the center crease; press. Fold the strips in half lengthwise again and press.

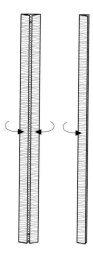

3. Wrap a prepared binding strip around each side edge of the project so that the raw edge of the project fits snugly against the center fold of the binding. Pin in place.

4. Using a spray box, spray the back of the buttons with temporary adhesive spray. Place the buttons on top of the binding, evenly spacing them about 1½" apart along each side. Drop the feed dogs on your sewing machine. With an open-toe embroidery foot, adjust the width of the zigzag stitch so that the needle enters each of the buttonholes. Zigzag five times to secure. Without cutting the thread, move to the next button.

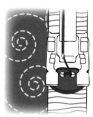

5. Cut the threads between the buttons. Add a drop of seam sealant to prevent the threads from unraveling.

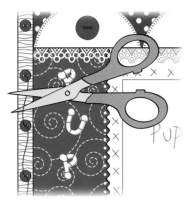

displaying your embellished beauty

Most of the projects in this book will be extremely lightweight. To hang a project on the wall, thread a needle with six strands of embroidery floss or pearl cotton and make a hanging loop through the backing fabric. Be sure to stitch through the backing fabric only. I use contrasting thread so that I can find it.

If there are no embellishments on the bottom edge, a small easel is perfect for display.

SUBJECT matter

The subject for a focal point in a project is limited only by your imagination. Once you decide on a theme, you have many ways to go about creating your quilt. You can start with a photo of people, animals, a vacation spot—or whatever you like. Other options for a focal point include embroidery, appliqué, a silk-screen design, or a preprinted novelty fabric.

When designing an embellished piece around a photo, here are a few considerations to keep in mind. Since the photo will be printed on fabric, it will lose some of its clarity, so choose a photo that's clear, crisp, and uncluttered. The photo should be a close-up shot of the subject, if possible. And the photo should have good contrast between the subject and the background.

This photo is not clear and crisp enough to print on fabric. The composition is good, but you can't see any of the details of the shed, and the horse blends into the shed. (Photo by Ann Davis.)

This snowy scene makes an amazing photo. However, although there's good contrast between the buggy and the background, there's very little of interest in the background and the buggy is distant. (Photo by Ann Davis.)

In this example, the previous photo is cropped to minimize the background. Now we have a great close-up, and there's nothing in the background distracting from the subject matter. (Photo by Ann Davis.)

Remember, you can crop, adjust, resize, and print a photo with a photo-editing program on your computer. Or you may find it easier to manipulate and resize the photo using your word-processing program. After choosing the desired size, print the photo on your fabric as described in "Printing Digitally" on page 17.

Is it important to match fabric to the photo? No. If you follow the guidelines in "Fabric Options" on page 22, you'll find that many combinations of fabrics will work with a photo. No "matching" is necessary. The examples on the opposite page show the exact same photo created with the same pattern used in the first project, "Celebrate Family" on page 32, with completely different fabrics and different embellishments. The fabrics are not meant to exclusively frame the photo, but to be an integral part of the project. They all look great. (These will be useful reference photos for embellishment ideas when you choose a project.)

Cheery, bright blue and teal fabrics, along with crowns at the top edge and a beaded bottom edge, create an eye-catching project.

Neutral colors, gold rickrack, metallic thread, beads, and ribbon accentuate the elegant look of this piece.

Thematic charms and fabrics give this project an Asian flavor.

A bold purple-black-and-teal geometric print makes a dramatic focus fabric. Rickrack embellished with sequins completes the design.

Create modern flair with fun colors and 3-D polka-dot flowers.

ELEGANTLY EMBELLISHED BEAUTIES

The projects on the following pages incorporate many of the techniques described in the previous sections. These projects are meant as a guide for your own experimentation. You may have trouble finding the exact fabrics or beads that I used. Feel free to choose fabrics and embellishments that you like. I created these projects from my heart, and they all mean something special to me. They may resonate with you, but if not, alter the projects to fit your personality. Choose a theme that means the most to you. Make the projects your own.

~ Cheryl

celebrate FAMILY

What could be more fun than to celebrate a family vacation or get-together by turning a photo into an embellished beauty? Print your photo on fabric and create a work of art with beautiful fabrics and embellishments. You can relive the time spent together as you stitch away.

Finished size: 10" x 8¼", excluding rickrack, ribbon, and dangling beads

WHAT YOU'LL NEED
materials

1 rectangle, 2½" x 10", of black-geometric batik for top border

1 rectangle, 3¼" x 10", of brown Burmese silk for bottom border

1 rectangle, 4" x 5½", of black-floral batik for side borders

1 rectangle, 5" x 9", of black print for binding

1 rectangle, 5" x 10", of cream batik for letters, plaque backing, and small circles

1 rectangle, 2" x 4", of taupe organza for outer circles

1 rectangle, 10" x 12", of fabric for backing

1 rectangle, 10" x 12", of low-loft batting

8½" x 11" sheet of inkjet-printable fabric for photo and plaque

1 rectangle, 5" x 12" of paper-backed fusible web

1 rectangle, 10" x 12", of heavyweight, double-sided fusible interfacing

embellishments

1 photo

11" of gold rickrack, ½" wide

3 yards of variegated silk ribbon, size 7 mm

Gold seed beads, size 11/0

4 brown seed beads, size 11/0

4 copper beads, size 3 mm

4 cream flat disc shell beads, ½" diameter

12 black seed beads, size 8/0

31 assorted metallic beads, size 6/0

4 metallic sequins, ¼" diameter

Black cotton embroidery floss

Burnt-orange rayon thread

Copper metallic thread

Black beading thread

tools and supplies

Hand towel

Small pair of pliers (optional)

embellishing tips

Add elegance and interest to your project by mixing fabrics with different fiber content. When using non-cotton fabric, lower the iron temperature and use a cotton pressing cloth. Otherwise, you may damage the non-cotton fabric.

ASSEMBLY

1. Following the manufacturer's instructions, print the photo on printable fabric. Trim the photo to measure 4" x 5½", which includes a ¼"-wide seam allowance on all sides.

2. Cut the black-floral batik rectangle in half to make two side borders, 2¾" x 4".

3. Arrange the photo fabric and the side, top, and bottom borders on the batting, right sides up. Join the side borders to the photo fabric using a ¼"-wide seam allowance and sewing through the fabric and batting. Add the top and bottom borders, again stitching through the fabric and batting. Press the fabrics open from the front after sewing each seam.

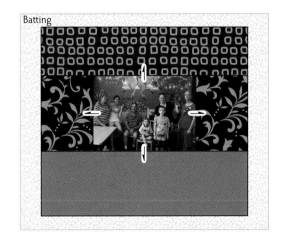

4. Quilt the side borders as desired.

EMBELLISHING

1. Referring to "Printing Digitally" on page 17, print the location and date (or desired words) on printable fabric. Apply fusible web to the wrong side of the printed fabric and trim the piece to measure 1¼" x 2". Be sure to follow the manufacturer's directions for the products you're using.

2. Refer to "Appliquéing Letters" on page 17. Using the patterns on page 35, the taupe organza for the outer circles, and the cream batik for the letters and small circles, prepare the letters and circles for fusible appliqué. Fuse the outer circles, and then the small circles to the side borders. Fuse the letters to the top border.

3. Cut a 2¼" x 3¼" cream-batik rectangle; apply fusible web to the wrong side, and then trim the rectangle to 2" x 3". Center the rectangle on the bottom border and fuse in place. Center and fuse the printed rectangle on top of the cream rectangle.

4. Using two strands of black cotton floss, whipstitch around the letters and smaller circles. Refer to "All the Stitches You'll Need" on page 14 as needed.

5. Using two strands of burnt-orange rayon thread, whipstitch around the larger circles and the cream plaque.

6. Use two strands of black cotton floss and the copper metallic thread to randomly fill the bottom border with chicken-scratch stitches. Add the gold seed beads.

7. Use beading thread to sew the sequins and brown seed beads to the corners of the printed rectangle. Add the cream flat beads and copper beads to the corners of the cream plaque.

FINISHING

1. Referring to "Assembling Your Project" on page 24, trim the top and bottom edges of the front piece. The piece should measure 8¾" from top to bottom. Sew the gold rickrack to the top edge, referring to "Rickrack" on page 20.

2. Trim the backing rectangle to measure 8¾" from top to bottom. With right sides together, sew the backing to the front piece along the top and bottom edges using a ¼"-wide seam allowance.

3. Measure between the top and bottom stitching lines and trim the interfacing to fit that measurement. Turn the piece right side out and insert the interfacing. Place the embellished front, right side down, on a hand towel and fuse the layers together. Trim the side edges, cutting through all the layers. The piece should measure 10" wide.

4. Cut the black print for binding in half lengthwise to make two 2½"-wide strips. Referring to "Double-Fold Binding" on page 26, make and attach the binding. Stitch the binding to the front using a machine blanket stitch.

5. Add two strands of ribbon through the seam along the bottom edge using the pliers to help pull the ribbon through, as needed. Then add the metallic beads and black seed beads; use gold seed beads as stop beads. Trim the ribbons to 2½" long.

Patterns are reversed for fusible appliqué.

Make 1 of each letter.

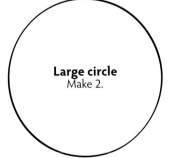

Small circle
Make 2.

Large circle
Make 2.

PUPS 4 sale

This crisp red-and-white piece was inspired by a sign at a farm stand during a trip to Pennsylvania Dutch country. Combining a vintage technique, such as redwork, with contemporary embellishing gives it a fresh and updated look.

Finished size: 14¾" x 16¼", including crown and jewels

WHAT YOU'LL NEED
materials

1 rectangle, 13" x 16", of white solid for embroidery panel and jewels

1 rectangle, 13" x 16", of white-and-red striped fabric for bottom border, crown, and binding

1 rectangle, 12" x 16", of red-with-white swirls fabric for side borders, crowns, and jewels

1 rectangle, 3" x 15", of red polka-dot fabric for top border

1 rectangle, 3" x 18", of white-on-white fabric for scallop appliqués

1 rectangle, 3" x 10", of red fabric for flourish appliqués

1 rectangle, 17" x 19", of fabric for backing

1 rectangle, 17" x 19", of low-loft batting

1 rectangle, 6" x 17", of paper-backed fusible web

1 rectangle, 17" x 19", of heavyweight, double-sided fusible interfacing

embellishments

15" of white lace trim, ½" wide

4 red buttons, ¾" diameter, for scallops (use vintage if you can find them)

18 red buttons, ⅜" diameter, for binding edge

58 white round, plastic pearl-like beads, size 4 mm

9 red faceted oblong beads, ⅜" long

9 clear seed beads, size 6/0

White foam letters, ¾" x ¾", to spell *PUPPIES* and *PURE JOY**

Red embroidery floss

White rayon floss

Red rayon thread

White beading thread

If you can't find white letters, you can use white spray paint to make the letters white.

tools and supplies

Blue water-soluble marker

Hand towel

Low-tack painter's tape, 1" wide

Rotary cutter with pinking blade

Safety pins

Spray box (optional, see page 24)

Temporary spray adhesive

Walking foot

embellishing tips
Spray paint and spray adhesive can make quite a mess. Turn a cardboard box into a spray box to contain the overspray.

CUTTING

From the white solid, cut:
1 rectangle, 10" x 11"
3 squares, 3" x 3"

From the red-with-white swirls fabric, cut:
2 rectangles, 3½" x 10¾"
2 squares, 4½" x 4½"
2 squares, 3" x 3"

From the white-and-red striped fabric, cut:
1 rectangle, 2¾" x 9¾"
2 rectangles, 2" x 14"
1 square, 5" x 5"

EMBROIDERED CENTER PANEL

1. Using a water-soluble marker, trace the embroidery design on page 41 onto the white-solid rectangle. Center the marked rectangle on top of the batting and pin in place using safety pins.

2. Use a walking foot and white thread to machine quilt a crosshatch pattern across the white rectangle; use painter's tape as a guide.

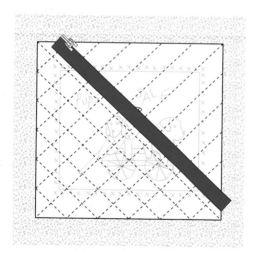

3. Use two strands of red embroidery floss to embroider the design. Use a running stitch for the dashed lines, a backstitch for the solid lines, and a cross-stitch for the Xs. When you're done stitching, remove the marks by quickly dunking the piece in water. Blot the piece between two layers of a towel and allow it to dry flat. Make sure the marks are completely removed before pressing or they'll become permanent.

ASSEMBLY

1. On the top edge, use a blue water-soluble marker to draw a placement line 1" above the running-stitch line. On the bottom edge, draw a line 3/4" below the running-stitch line. On each side, draw a placement line 1/2" from the running-stitch line. The placement lines will be hidden in the seam allowance.

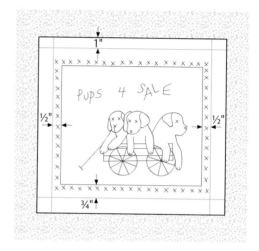

2. Align one edge of the 2¾" x 9¾" white-and-red striped rectangle with the marked line along the bottom edge, right sides together. Join the pieces using a ¼"-wide seam allowance and stitching through the fabric and batting. Open the striped fabric and press from the front.

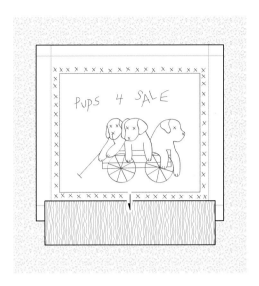

3. Iron a ½"-wide strip of fusible web along one edge of each red-with-white swirls rectangle. On each rectangle, use a rotary cutter with a pinking blade to trim ¼" from the fused edge. Remove the paper backing.

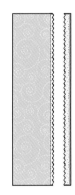

4. Position the trimmed rectangles on top of the center panel, just covering the marked line. Press to fuse in place.

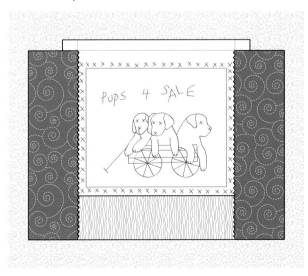

5. Align one edge of the lace trim with the marked line along the top edge. Pin in place.

6. Using fusible web and the scallop pattern on page 40, prepare four white-on-white scallops for fusible appliqué. Fold the red polka-dot rectangle in half to create a centerline. Place a scallop on each side of the line; then place a scallop on each side of the center scallops as shown. Fuse the scallops in place.

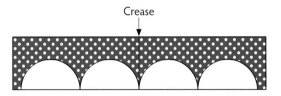

Crease

7. Align the red polka-dot rectangle with the edge of the lace, right sides together. Join the pieces using a ¼"-wide seam allowance and stitching through the fabric, lace, and batting. Press the red rectangle open from the front, pressing the lace toward the center.

8. Using red thread, machine blanket-stitch around the scallops, sewing through all the layers.

EMBELLISHING

Refer to "All the Stitches You'll Need" on page 14 as needed.

1. Using fusible web and the flourish pattern on page 40, prepare one flourish and one reversed flourish from the red fabric. Fuse the flourishes to the bottom border as shown in the photo on page 36. Use red rayon thread and a whipstitch to stitch the flourishes in place. Add the white pearl-like beads using white beading thread.

2. Use the white rayon floss to make about 35 French knots along each pinked edge on the side borders.

3. Place the white foam letters along the side borders as shown in the photo. Remove the backing paper to temporarily position the letters. Use red rayon thread to whipstitch the letters in place.

4. Using a spray box, spray the back of the ¾"-diameter red buttons with temporary adhesive spray so you can adhere them in place. Attach a button to each scallop with red rayon thread.

FINISHING

1. Refer to "Crowns" and "Jewels" on page 19. Make one crown using the 5" white-and-red striped square. Make two crowns using the 4½" red-with-white swirls squares. Make two jewels using the 3" red-with-white swirls squares. Make three jewels using the white squares.

2. Referring to "Assembling Your Project" on page 24, trim the top and bottom edges of the front piece. The piece should measure 13¼" from top to bottom. Aligning the raw edges with the white-and-red striped crown in the center, baste the three crowns to the top edge. Baste the jewels to the bottom edge, alternating the red and white jewels as shown in the photo on page 36.

3. Trim the backing rectangle to measure 13¼" from top to bottom. With right sides together, sew the backing to the front piece along the top and bottom edges using a ¼"-wide seam allowance.

4. Measure between the top and bottom stitching lines and trim the interfacing to fit that measurement. Turn the piece right side out and insert the interfacing. Place the embellished front, right side down, on a hand towel and fuse the layers together. Trim the side edges, cutting through all the layers. The piece should measure 14¾" wide.

5. Referring to "Button Binding" on page 28, make and attach the binding using the red-and-white striped fabric and the ⅜"-diameter red buttons.

6. Create a trio of beads using a clear seed bead, a red faceted bead, and a white round bead as a stop bead. Use beading thread to sew the beads to the point on each jewel and between the jewels as shown.

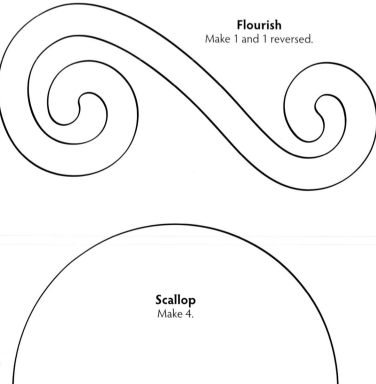

Flourish
Make 1 and 1 reversed.

Scallop
Make 4.

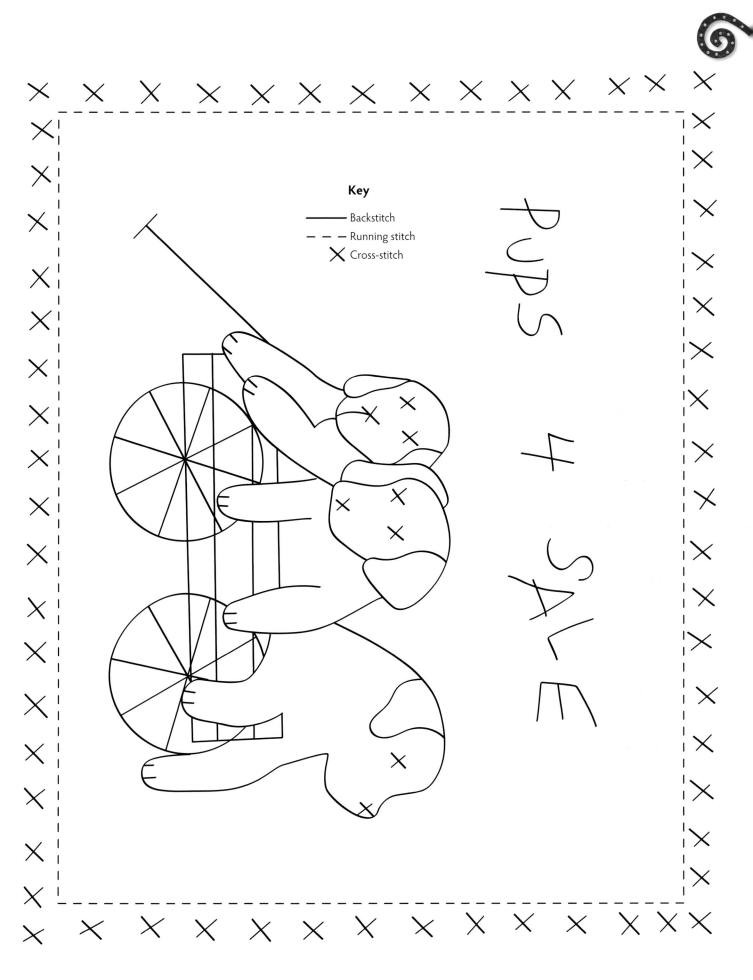

Key

—— Backstitch

- - - Running stitch

✕ Cross-stitch

PUPS 4 SALE

UFO fun!

Turning a pieced block from an unfinished project (UFO) or an experiment into an embellished beauty is as easy as finding a fun appliqué. Appliqué these cheerful birds, add embellishments, and you'll have a finished piece in no time.

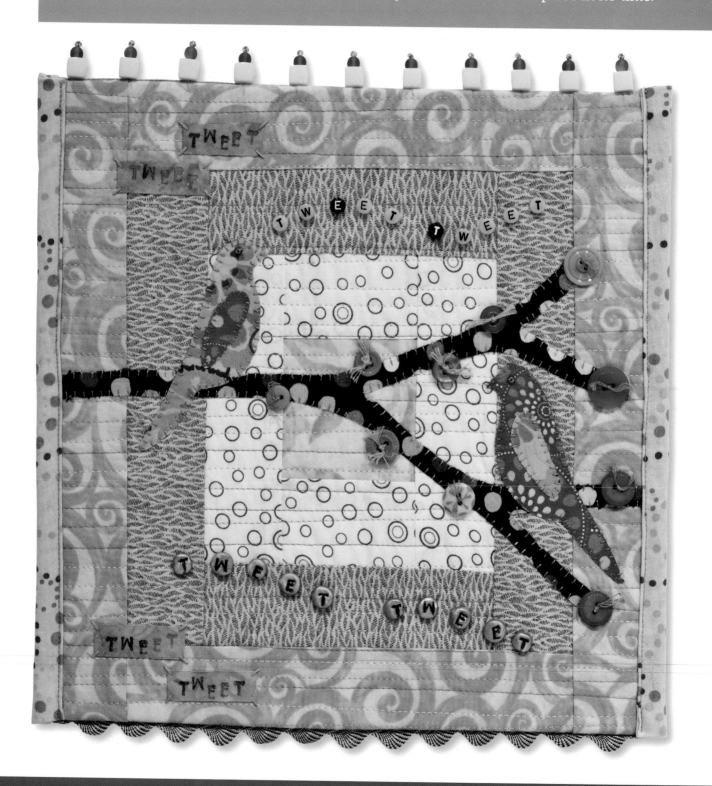

Finished size: 11" x 12", excluding rickrack and beads

WHAT YOU'LL NEED
materials

1 leftover block, 12½" x 12½"*

1 rectangle, 8" x 12", of brown polka-dot fabric for branch appliqué

1 rectangle, 4" x 6", of bright-pink fabric for bird appliqué

1 rectangle, 4" x 6", of green-print fabric for bird appliqué

1 square, 3" x 3", of orange fabric for *TWEET* tags

2 rectangles, 2½" x 12", of light-blue fabric for binding

1 rectangle, 13" x 15", of fabric for backing

1 rectangle, 13" x 15", of low-loft batting

1 square, 12" x 12", of paper-backed fusible web

1 rectangle, 13" x 15", of heavyweight, double-sided fusible interfacing

If you don't have a leftover block, make a simple block similar to the one used in this project.

embellishments

12" of green rickrack, ½" or ⅝" wide

10 orange buttons, ⅜" to ¾" diameter

2 purple seed beads, size 11/0, for bird eyes

2 sets of black and white letter beads, ¼" diameter, to spell *TWEET*

11 white cube glass beads, size 8 mm

11 blue round beads, size 6 mm

11 translucent green seed beads, size 8/0

Chartreuse cotton embroidery floss

Rust rayon thread

Variegated blue rayon thread

White beading thread

White polymer clay

tools and supplies

Alphabet rubber stamps, ¼"

Black permanent marker, fine tipped

Black stamp pad

Gold metallic spray paint

Hand towel

Open-toe embroidery foot (optional)

Polymer-clay supplies

Safety pins

Seam sealant

Spray box (optional, see page 24)

Walking foot

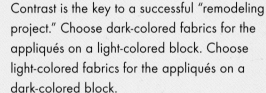

embellishing tip

Contrast is the key to a successful "remodeling project." Choose dark-colored fabrics for the appliqués on a light-colored block. Choose light-colored fabrics for the appliqués on a dark-colored block.

APPLIQUÉ

1. Center the leftover block on top of the batting and secure with a few safety pins. Use variegated blue rayon thread and a walking foot to machine quilt horizontal straight lines.

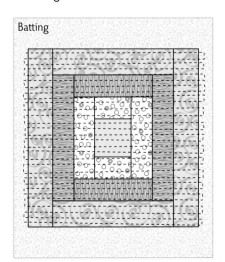

Batting

2. Using fusible web and the patterns on page 45, prepare the bird and branch appliqués using the appropriate fabrics. Fuse the branch to the block. Use a whipstitch and variegated blue rayon thread to stitch the branch in place. Be sure to follow the manufacturer's directions for the product you're using.

3. Fuse the birds to the branch and add the wings. Whipstitch the appliqués in place using rust rayon thread.

EMBELLISHING

1. Referring to "Polymer-Clay Embellishments" on page 10 and using the white polymer clay, make 10 pea-sized balls. Use the alphabet rubber stamps to make two sets of beads that spell TWEET. After baking, paint the beads with gold metallic spray paint. Darken the letters with a black marker. Attach the beads to the background using beading thread.

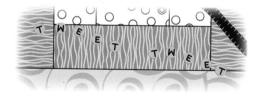

2. To make the TWEET tags, press fusible web to the wrong side of the orange square. Cut the fused square into four ½" x 1⅝" rectangles. Use the alphabet rubber stamps and black stamp pad to stamp TWEET onto each rectangle. Fuse the rectangles to the background. Tack down the corners of each rectangle using three strands of chartreuse embroidery floss and a whipstitch.

3. Add a purple seed bead to each bird for the eye.

4. Attach the orange buttons with three strands of the chartreuse cotton embroidery floss. Secure with a drop of seam sealant.

5. Use beading thread to attach the black and white letter beads spelling TWEET TWEET.

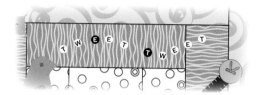

FINISHING

1. Referring to "Assembling Your Project" on page 24, trim the top and bottom edges of the front piece. The piece should measure 12½" from top to bottom. Sew the green rickrack to the bottom edge, referring to "Rickrack" on page 20.

2. Trim the backing rectangle to measure 12½" from top to bottom. With right sides together, sew the backing to the front piece along the top and bottom edges using a ¼"-wide seam allowance.

3. Measure between the top and bottom stitching lines and trim the interfacing to fit that measurement. Turn the piece right side out and insert the interfacing. Place the embellished front, right side down, on a hand towel and fuse the layers together. Trim the side edges, cutting through all the layers. The piece should measure 11" wide.

4. Referring to "Double-Fold Binding" on page 26 and using the light-blue rectangles, make and attach the binding. Stitch the binding to the front, sewing a straight line close to the folded edge.

5. Create a trio of beads using a white cube bead, a blue round bead, and a green seed bead as a stop bead. Use beading thread to add each trio of beads along the top edge, evenly spacing them as shown.

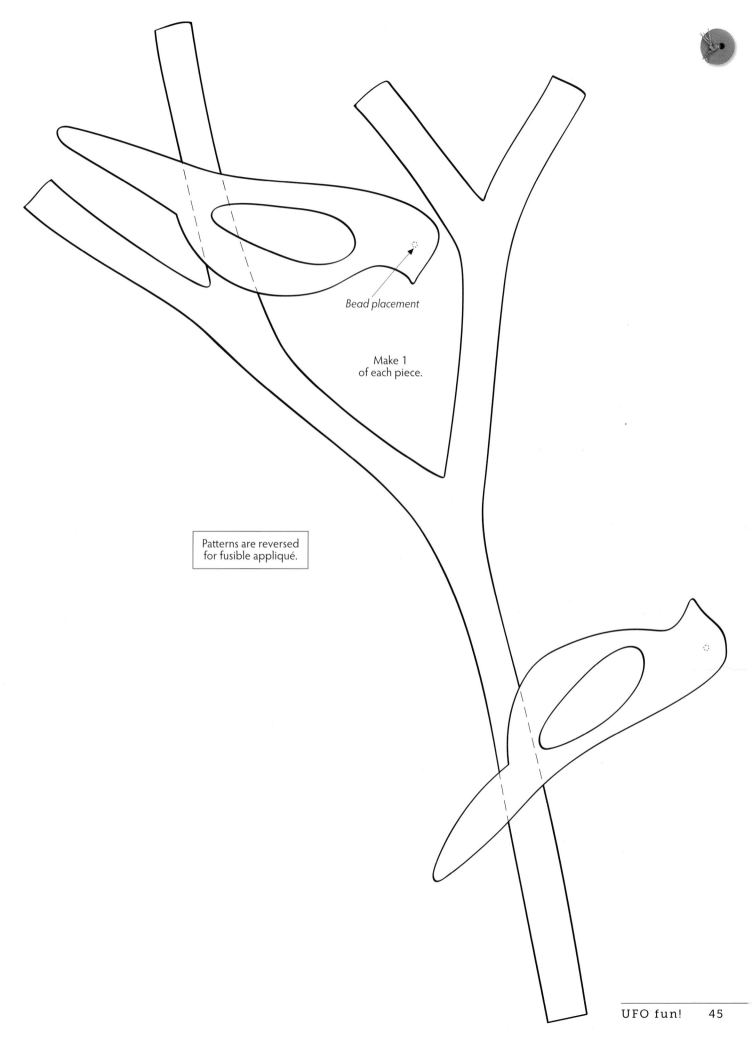

Bead placement

Make 1
of each piece.

Patterns are reversed
for fusible appliqué.

XOXOX

XOXOX means hugs and kisses. You can translate this affection in traditional Valentine's Day colors or choose your favorite color palette. This is a great project to use odds and ends of your beads and buttons.

Finished size: 9" x 11½", including crown and excluding dangling beads

WHAT YOU'LL NEED
materials

1 square, 10" x 10", of red solid for borders

1 rectangle, 8" x 10", of white-with-red dots fabric for center panel and crowns

1 rectangle, 9" x 12", of red plaid for heart, crown, and binding

1 rectangle, 5" x 7", of white-with-red swirls fabric for letter appliqués

1 rectangle, 11" x 12", of fabric for backing

1 rectangle, 11" x 12", of low-loft batting

1 rectangle, 9" x 16", of paper-backed fusible web

1 rectangle, 11" x 12", of heavyweight, double-sided fusible interfacing

embellishments

28 white buttons, ⅜" to ½" diameter

8 white teardrop beads, size 15 mm

8 red seed beads, size 6/0

8 white seed beads, size 8/0

Assorted red, white, pink, and clear beads

Red pearl cotton, size 8

White pearl cotton, size 8

Red rayon thread

White beading thread

White polymer clay

tools and supplies

Alphabet rubber stamps, ½"

Gold spray paint

Hand towel

Polymer-clay supplies

Rotary cutter with pinking blade

Safety pins

Seam sealant

Spray box (optional, see page 24)

Spray can of clear acrylic sealer

embellishing tip

Any type of stamp can be used with polymer clay to create your personal embellishment. Create, bake, paint, and seal.

CUTTING

From the white-with-red dots fabric, cut:
1 rectangle, 5½" x 7"
2 squares, 3" x 3"

From the red solid, cut:
2 rectangles, 2¼" x 7"
2 rectangles, 2¼" x 9"

From the red plaid, cut:
1 rectangle, 2" x11"
1 rectangle, 4½" x 5½"
1 square, 3½" x 3½"

ASSEMBLY

1. Center the white-with-red dots rectangle on top of the batting and secure with safety pins. Use red pearl cotton and a big stitch to hand quilt straight lines. Refer to "All the Stitches You'll Need" on page 14 as needed.

2. Sew the 2¼" x 7" red-solid rectangles to opposite sides of the quilted rectangle using a ¼"-wide seam allowance and stitching through the fabric and batting. In the same way, add the 2¼" x 9" red-solid rectangles to the top and bottom edges. Press the fabrics open from the front after sewing each seam.

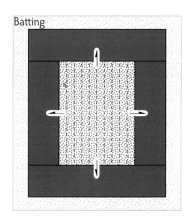

3. Refer to "Appliquéing Letters" on page 17. Using the patterns on page 49 and the white-with-red swirls fabric, prepare four of each letter for fusible appliqué. Fuse the letters to the borders as shown in the photo on page 46. Be sure to follow the manufacturer's directions for the product you're using.

4. Using the heart pattern on page 49 and the 4½" x 5½" plaid rectangle, prepare one plaid heart for fusible appliqué. Center the heart on the white-with-red dots rectangle and fuse in place.

EMBELLISHING

1. Refer to "Polymer-Clay Embellishments" on page 10. Start with a ½" ball of white polymer clay, flatten the ball, and then use the alphabet stamps to spell XOXOX. Make a hole in each corner. After baking, spray paint the plaque with gold paint. When the gold paint is completely dry, spray the plaque with clear acrylic sealer.

2. Use red pearl cotton to attach the white buttons around the heart.

3. Using two strands of red rayon thread, whipstitch around the letters. Refer to "All the Stitches You'll Need" as needed.

4. Use beading thread to randomly sew the assorted beads in the borders. *Do not* place any beads within ½" of the outer edge.

FINISHING

1. Referring to "Crowns" on page 19, make one crown using the red-plaid square. Make two crowns using the white-with-red dots squares.

2. Referring to "Assembling Your Project" on page 24, trim the top and bottom edges of the front piece. The piece should measure 10½" from top to bottom. Aligning the raw edges, and with the red-plaid crown in the center, baste the three crowns to the top edge.

3. Trim the backing rectangle to measure 10½" from top to bottom. With right sides together, sew the backing to the front piece along the top and bottom edges using a ¼"-wide seam allowance.

4. Measure between the top and bottom stitching lines and trim the interfacing to fit that measurement. Turn the piece right side out and insert the interfacing. Place the embellished front, right side down, on a hand towel and fuse the layers together. Trim the side edges, cutting through all the layers. The piece should measure 9" wide.

5. Apply fusible web to the wrong side of the 2" x 11" red-plaid rectangle. Using a rotary cutter with a pinking blade, cut the fused rectangle in half lengthwise to make two 1"-wide strips. Referring to "Fusible Binding" on page 27, attach the binding.

6. Use white pearl cotton to attach the XOXOX plaque in the center of the heart. Tie the thread tails in a square knot, trim the thread, and add a drop of seam sealant to each knot.

7. Create a trio of beads using a white teardrop bead, a red seed bead, and a white seed bead as a stop bead. Use beading thread to sew the beads to the bottom edge as shown.

Patterns are reversed
for fusible appliqué.

Make 4 of each letter.

Heart
Make 1.

tranquility TREE

Nature provides the backdrop for a beautifully tranquil piece. Free-motion quilting is used to simultaneously quilt the tree and add the smaller branches. This is a great place to experiment with thread-painting techniques, whether you're new to them or experienced.

Finished size: 8½" x 12½", including jewels at bottom and excluding rickrack at top

WHAT YOU'LL NEED
materials

1 rectangle, 8" x 10", of multicolored fabric for arched top and jewels

1 rectangle, 8" x 9", of terra-cotta batik for side borders and jewels

1 rectangle, 6" x 12", of green batik for left side border and binding

1 rectangle, 2½" x 8½", of navy-with-leaves batik for bottom border

1 rectangle, 5" x 6½", of blue fabric for sky

1 rectangle, 5" x 6½", of brown fabric for tree

1 rectangle, 2½" x 4", of navy batik for left side border

1 rectangle, 2" x 5", of gold batik for *Tranquility* plaque

1 rectangle, 10" x 15", of fabric for backing

1 rectangle, 10" x 15", of low-loft batting

1 rectangle, 8" x 10", of paper-backed fusible web

1 rectangle, 10" x 15", of heavyweight, double-sided fusible interfacing

embellishments

½ yard of green rickrack, ½" or ⅝" wide

9" of brown rickrack, ½" or ⅝" wide

3 leaf buttons or beads, ⅝" diameter

6 off-white wooden disc beads, size 10 mm

17 teal seed beads, size 8/0

17 copper sequins, size 6 mm

Dragonfly brass charm, ½" diameter

Light-blue rayon thread

Brown rayon thread, 30 weight, for quilting tree branches

Blue-gray, maroon, and navy cotton embroidery floss

Green rayon floss

Light-gray beading thread

tools and supplies

Blue water-soluble marker or chalk marker

Hand towel

Lunch plate, 8½" diameter (or 8½" circle)

Open-toe darning foot

Rotary cutter with pinking blade

Safety pins

design tips
Choosing fabrics with low contrast imparts a feeling of calm and harmony to a quilt.

cutting
From the multicolored fabric, cut:
1 rectangle, 4" x 8½"
3 squares, 3" x 3"

From the terra-cotta batik, cut:
1 rectangle, 2" x 6½"
2 squares, 3" x 3"
1 rectangle, 2½" x 4"

From the green batik, cut:
1 rectangle, 2" x 11"
1 rectangle, 2½" x 4"

CREATING THE CENTER PANEL

1. Center the blue-sky rectangle on the batting and secure it with a few safety pins.

2. Use two strands of light-blue rayon thread and a big stitch to hand quilt the sky rectangle. Refer to "All the Stitches You'll Need" on page 14 as needed.

Batting

3. Using fusible web and the pattern on page 55, prepare the tree for fusible appliqué. Align the bottom of the tree with the bottom edge of the sky fabric and fuse in place. Be sure to follow the manufacturer's directions for the product you're using.

4. Using an open-toe darning foot and brown rayon thread, free-motion quilt the tree and branches. Be sure to use the same thread color in the bobbin as you're using on the top of your machine.

✳ free-motion quilting tips

When stitching the tree, the goal is to quilt the tree and add the little branches at the same time. It's all right to stitch on top of previous stitches and cross over them as well, since that's the best way to build up the design. Drop the feed dogs on your sewing machine and lower the top tension. You'll use the sewing machine to "draw" on your quilt.

1. Start at the bottom of the tree and travel up to the first branch on the right side and out to the end of the branch, adding smaller branches in a Y shape. As you travel back down the branch, add smaller branches on the other side, until you're at the beginning of the branch again.

2. Continue up the tree to the next branch. In the same manner as before, travel along the branch, adding smaller branches on both sides.

3. Continue up the tree, stitching each branch as you go, until you reach the top branch. Stitch down the center to the bottom of the tree.

4. In the same way, travel up the left side of the tree, stitching each branch and adding smaller branches. When you reach the top, stitch down the center to the base of the tree.

5. Repeat steps 1–4, stitching each branch again and going over the smaller branches.

6. Repeat the stitching again. This time stitch through the center of each branch and down through the middle of the trunk. You don't need to stitch the smaller branches a third time.

ASSEMBLY

1. From each of the 2½" x 4" terra-cotta, navy-batik, and green-batik rectangles, cut a 2½" square. Using the remaining rectangle of each fabric, apply a 1½" x 2½" rectangle of fusible web to the wrong side of each rectangle. Cut a 1¼" square and a ¾" square from each fabric. You should have two fused squares and one 2½" square of each fabric.

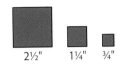

2½" 1¼" ¾"

2. Alternating the terra-cotta, navy, and green fabrics, place a medium square on top of a large square as shown and fuse them together. Center and fuse a small square on top of the medium square. Make three fused squares.

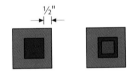

½"

3. Sew the three squares from step 2 together to make the left side border; press. Sew the border to the left side of the stitched center panel using a ¼"-wide seam allowance and stitching through the fabric and batting.

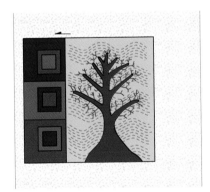

4. Sew the 2" x 6½" terra-cotta rectangle to the right side of the center panel, stitching through the fabric and batting. Press the rectangle open from the front. Machine quilt several wavy lines from top to bottom.

5. Sew the navy-with-leaves rectangle to the bottom of the center panel, stitching through the fabric and batting. Press the rectangle open from the front. Machine quilt wavy lines from side to side.

6. Align and baste the brown rickrack along the top edge, referring to "Rickrack" on page 20. Place the multicolored rectangle on top of the rickrack with the top edges aligned. Join the pieces, sewing through all the layers. Press the rectangle open from the front.

7. Center an 8½" plate on the top border, aligned with the right and left sides and about ¼" from the top edge. Draw a line around the plate with a water-soluble marker or a chalk marker to form an arch. Cut on the line, trimming away the excess fabric and batting.

¼"

EMBELLISHING

Refer to "All the Stitches You'll Need" as needed.

1. In the left border, use two strands of cotton floss as shown in the photo to whipstitch around the edges of the fused squares in the left border. Then sew a leaf button in the center of each small square.

2. Sew the off-white disc beads to the right border using two strands of blue-gray cotton floss, making sure the beads are at least ½" from the outer edge.

3. Use beading thread to add the sequins and seed beads to the top border, making sure the beads are at least ½" from the outer edge.

4. Referring to "Printing Digitally" on page 17, print *Tranquility* on the right side of the gold-batik rectangle. I used a size 48 Papyrus font, but you can use the font of your choice. Iron fusible web on the wrong side of the gold rectangle and trim it to measure 1" x 3¾". Fuse the gold rectangle to the bottom border, placing it about ½" from the bottom and right edges. Using three strands of maroon cotton floss, whipstitch around the edges of the rectangle.

5. Refer to the tree pattern on page 55 for placement guidance. Using green rayon floss, add French knots to the ends of each small stitched branch.

FINISHING

1. Referring to "Jewels" on page 19, make three jewels using the multicolored squares. Make two jewels using the terra-cotta squares.

2. Referring to "Assembling Your Project" on page 24, trim the bottom edge of the front piece. Aligning the raw edges, baste the five jewels to the bottom edge, alternating them as shown in the photo on page 50.

3. Pin the green rickrack on the top edge, following the curve, and baste ⅛" from the edge.

4. Place the front piece on top of the backing rectangle, right sides together, with the bottom edges aligned. Pin the pieces together, making sure the backing piece is on the bottom. Using a ¼"-wide seam allowance, sew along the curved edge and the bottom edge. Trim the top edge of the backing to match the curve. *Do not* turn the piece right side out or trim the sides yet.

5. Place the piece from step 4 on top of the interfacing and align the bottom edge with the edge of the interfacing. Trim the interfacing to match the curved top edge. Then trim off a ¼" seam allowance from the top and bottom edges.

6. Turn the piece from step 4 right side out and insert the interfacing. Place the embellished front, right side down, on a hand towel and fuse the layers together. Trim the side edges, cutting through all the layers. The piece should measure 8½" wide.

7. Apply fusible web to the wrong side of the 2" x 11" green-batik rectangle. Using a rotary cutter with a pinking blade, cut the fused rectangle in half lengthwise to make two 1"-wide strips. Referring to "Fusible Binding" on page 27, attach the binding.

8. Hang the dragonfly charm from the bottom-left corner.

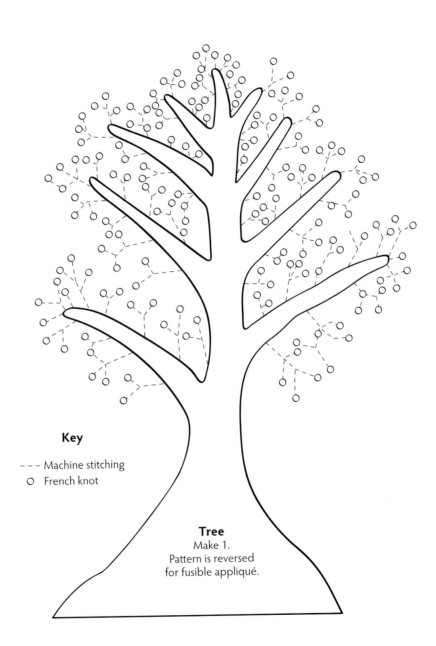

Key

- – – Machine stitching
- O French knot

Tree
Make 1.
Pattern is reversed
for fusible appliqué.

ORANGE crush

Make this fun, happy project, with the peekaboo door, to surprise a modern couple in love. The surprise? Their photo is hiding underneath the flap.

Finished size: 11" x 26½", including crown and jewels

WHAT YOU'LL NEED
materials

1 rectangle, 7" x 33", of orange floral for right side panel, center crown, and jewel

1 rectangle, 10" x 23", of orange polka-dot fabric for jewel and binding

1 rectangle, 10" x 20", of yellow polka-dot fabric for center panel, crowns, jewel, and flower-center appliqués

1 rectangle, 10" x 17", of salmon dupioni silk for left side panel, crowns, and appliquéd squares

1 rectangle, 10" x 11", of white-with-orange polka-dot fabric for Peekaboo block, flower-petal appliqués, and letter backgrounds

1 rectangle, 5" x 12", of red tone-on-tone fabric for letter and flower-petal appliqués

1 rectangle, 8" x 12", of orange-with-pink swirls fabric for top border and peekaboo flap

1 rectangle, 13" x 23", of backing fabric

1 rectangle, 13" x 23", of low-loft batting

1 rectangle, 3" x 4", of inkjet-printable fabric

⅜ yard of 17"-wide paper-backed fusible web

embellishments

1 photo

12 translucent white flower buttons, ½" diameter

36 orange seed beads, size 11/0

4 orange elongated glass beads, size 12 mm

4 pearl disc beads, size 8 mm

2 translucent orange seed beads, size 6/0

8 brass washers, ½" diameter

2 brass heart charms, ¼" diameter

1 brass heart charm, ¾" diameter

Pink rayon thread

Gold metallic thread

Purple metallic thread

White beading thread

tools and supplies

Blue water-soluble pen

Freezer paper

Open-toe embroidery foot (optional)

Safety pins

Walking foot (optional)

CUTTING

From the orange floral, cut:
1 rectangle, 5½" x 18½"
1 square, 5" x 5"
1 rectangle, 4½" x 6"

From the salmon dupioni silk, cut:
1 rectangle, 5½" x 15"
2 squares, 3" x 3"
1 rectangle, 2½" x 4½"

From the yellow polka-dot fabric, cut:
1 rectangle, 3½" x 18½"
2 squares, 4" x 4"
1 rectangle, 4½" x 6"

From the white-with-orange polka-dot fabric, cut:
2 rectangles, 1½" x 5½"
2 squares, 2" x 2"
1 rectangle, 5" x 7"

From the orange-with-pink swirls fabric, cut:
1 rectangle, 3" x 11"
1 rectangle, 3" x 5"

From the orange polka-dot fabric, cut:
2 rectangles, 2¼" x 21½"
1 rectangle, 4½" x 6"

LEFT PANEL

1. Use a water-soluble pen to lightly trace the vine pattern on page 62 onto the 5½" x 15" salmon silk rectangle, overlapping the two sections at the registration mark to make the entire design. Place the traced rectangle on the left side of the batting, 1" from the outer edge, and secure with a few safety pins. Use gold thread and a backstitch to hand embroider the vine design. Refer to "All the Stitches You'll Need" on page 14 as needed. After the design is completely stitched, remove any visible traced lines by lightly dabbing with a damp cloth.

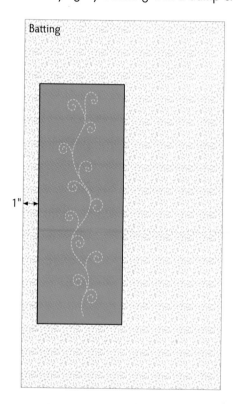

2. Following the manufacturer's instructions, print the photo on printable fabric. Trim the photo to measure 2" x 2½", which includes a ¼"-wide seam allowance on all sides.

3. Sew white-with-orange polka-dot squares to opposite sides of the photo; press. Sew 1½" x 5½" white-with-orange polka-dot rectangles to the top and bottom edges to complete the Peekaboo block. Press.

4. For the flap, apply fusible web to the wrong side of the 3" x 5" orange-with-pink swirls rectangle following the manufacturer's directions. Remove the paper backing. Fold the rectangle in half, wrong sides together, to make a 2½" x 3" rectangle. Press and trim the rectangle to measure 2" x 2½". Straight stitch around, stitching close to the edges.

5. Place the flap on top of the Peekaboo block, with the edge of the flap ¼" above the top edge of the photo. Stitch ⅛" from the top edge, and then sew a second line of stitching close to the edge.

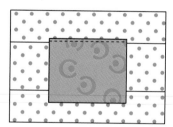

6. With right sides together, sew the Peekaboo block to the bottom of the embroidered silk rectangle using a ¼"-wide seam allowance and stitching through fabric and the batting. Press the block open from the front.

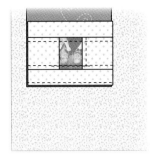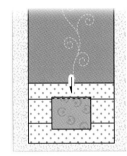

RIGHT PANEL

1. Following the manufacturer's instructions, apply fusible web to the wrong side of the 5" x 7" white-with-orange polka-dot rectangle. Cut seven 1½" x 2" rectangles from the fused rectangle. *Do not* remove the paper backing.

2. Refer to "Appliquéing Letters" on page 17. Using fusible web and the patterns on page 63, prepare the red tone-on-tone letters for fusible appliqué. Cut out each letter and fuse it in the center of a rectangle from step 1. Remove the paper backing. Using pink rayon thread, whipstitch around the letters. Refer to "All the Stitches You'll Need" as needed.

3. Place the appliquéd rectangles on the 5½" x 18½" orange-floral rectangle, aligning them 1½" from the right edge and about ⅜" apart. Fuse the rectangles in place. Use gold thread to whipstitch around the rectangles.

4. Place the orange-floral rectangle on top of the batting, next to the embroidered silk rectangle. The long sides of the rectangles should be touching, but not overlapped, and the top and bottom edges should be aligned. Pin the rectangles in place. Baste around each rectangle, stitching about ⅛" from the raw edges.

1½"

ASSEMBLY

1. Cut a 3½" x 18½" piece of freezer paper. Place the freezer paper on a cutting mat, shiny side down, and use a rotary cutter to cut gentle curves along each long side.

2. With the shiny side facing up, place the trimmed freezer paper on the wrong side of the 3½" x 18½" yellow polka-dot fabric as shown and pin in place. Trim the fabric to match the curves, leaving a ¼"-wide seam allowance beyond the edges of the paper. Clip the fabric along the inside curves.

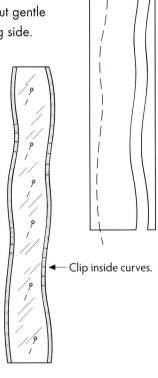

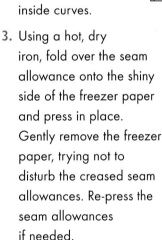
← Clip inside curves.

3. Using a hot, dry iron, fold over the seam allowance onto the shiny side of the freezer paper and press in place. Gently remove the freezer paper, trying not to disturb the creased seam allowances. Re-press the seam allowances if needed.

4. Center the prepared strip on top of the batting, covering the line where the left and right panels meet as shown. The top and bottom edges should all be aligned. Pin the center strip in place and machine blanket-stitch along both folded edges using pink rayon thread.

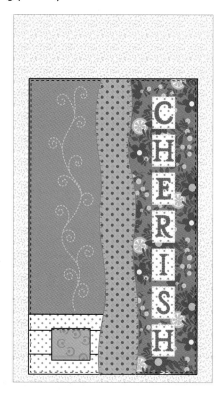

5. With right sides together and side edges aligned, sew the 3" x 11" orange-with-pink swirls rectangle to the top of the piece using a ¼"-wide seam allowance and stitching through the fabric and batting. Press the rectangle open from the front.

6. Using fusible web and the patterns on page 63, prepare eight red tone-on-tone petals, four white-with-orange polka-dot petals, and three yellow polka-dot flower centers for fusible appliqué. Fuse the appliqués to the top border and whipstitch in place using the pink rayon thread.

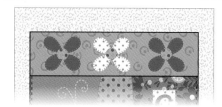

Appliqué placement

EMBELLISHING

1. Press a 2½" x 4½" rectangle of fusible web to the 2½" x 4½" salmon silk rectangle following the manufacturer's directions. From the fused rectangle, cut eight 1" squares. Referring to the photo on page 56 for placement guidance, fuse the squares to the yellow polka-dot strip.

2. Using purple metallic thread, make eight French knots around the edges of each silk square. Refer to "All the Stitches You'll Need" as needed. Center a brass washer on each square. Using pink rayon thread, whipstitch the washers in place as shown.

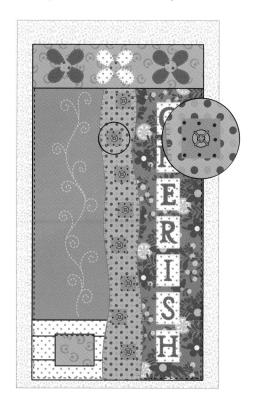

3. Using white beading thread and three orange seed beads, attach the flower buttons to the embroidered panel as shown.

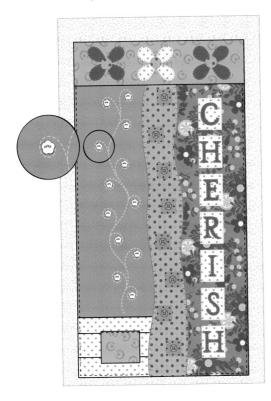

FINISHING

1. Machine quilt the orange-floral strip and the top border behind the appliqué flowers.

2. Referring to "Crowns" on page 19, make one crown using the orange-floral square. Make two crowns using the yellow polka-dot squares and two crowns using the salmon silk squares. Use the 4½" x 6" rectangles of orange floral, orange polka-dot fabric, and yellow polka-dot fabric to make one elongated jewel from each rectangle (three total).

3. Referring to "Assembling Your Project" on page 24, trim the top and bottom edges of the front piece. The piece should measure 21" from top to bottom. Starting with the orange-floral crown in the center, position the silk crowns and yellow polka-dot crowns along the top edge with the raw edges aligned; baste the crowns in place.

4. Aligning the raw edges, baste the jewels to the bottom edge. Refer to the photo on page 56 for placement guidance.

5. Trim the backing rectangle to measure 21" from top to bottom. With right sides together, sew the backing to the front piece along the top and bottom edges using a ¼"-wide seam allowance.

6. Turn the piece right side out. Trim the side edges, cutting through all the layers. The piece should measure 11" wide.

7. Refer to "Double-Fold Binding" on page 26 and use the 2½" x 21½" orange polka-dot rectangles to make and attach the binding. Stitch the binding to the front, sewing a straight line close to the folded edge.

8. Topstitch along the top and bottom edges. Quilt through all the layers by stitching in the ditch across the bottom of the top border, along the edges of the yellow polka-dot strip, and across the top of the Peekaboo block.

9. Embellish the jewels with beads and heart charms as shown.

Align registration marks to make complete pattern.

← Registration mark

← Registration mark

Make 1 of each letter.

Flower petal
Make 12.

Flower center
Make 3.

CHERISH

from the bottom of MY HEART

These houses pay homage to heartfelt feelings. The blue and purple batiks seem to come from a place of joy. When you've run out of room on your walls, this project can stand on its own and be displayed anywhere.

Finished size: 22½" x 10½", excluding buttons

WHAT YOU'LL NEED
materials

1 rectangle, 5½" x 8" *each*, of 5 assorted batiks for houses

1 rectangle, 4½" x 5½" *each*, of 5 assorted batiks for roofs

1 rectangle, 4" x 7" *each*, of 5 assorted batiks for heart appliqués

1 rectangle, 4" x 6", of light-value fabric for tags

1 rectangle, 5" x 16", of fabric for binding

1 rectangle, 12" x 24", of fabric for backing

1 rectangle, 14" x 32", of low-loft batting

½ yard of 17"-wide paper-backed fusible web

1 rectangle, 12" x 24", of heavyweight, double-sided fusible interfacing

embellishments

6"-long piece *each* of 5 assorted colors of rickrack, ½" or ⅝" wide

1 yard of blue velvet ribbon, ⅜" wide

1 yard *each* of 5 assorted ribbons or decorative threads (such as 4 mm silk ribbon and 3 mm metallic ribbon)

38 to 40 white oval beads, 8 mm long

25 purple sequins, size 6 mm

32 green square sequins, size 4 mm

Gold seed beads, size 11/0

Light-blue seed beads, size 11/0

Metallic or rayon threads to match heart appliqués

Light-gray beading thread

White beading thread

Purple polymer clay

Light-blue metallic polymer clay

tools and supplies

Alphabet rubber stamps, ¼"

Black dye-based stamp pad

Blue water-soluble marker

Open-toe embroidery foot

Parchment paper

Template plastic, 8½" x 11" sheet

Walking foot

PREPARING THE HOUSES

1. Cut the batting into five 6" x 14" pieces. Place one 5½" x 8" batik rectangle on top of one piece of batting, with the bottom edge of the rectangle about ½" from the bottom edge of the batting. Use a walking foot to machine quilt straight lines. In the same manner, layer and quilt the four remaining house rectangles.

½"

2. Using fusible web and the heart pattern on page 69, trace five hearts onto fusible web. Following the manufacturer's instructions, fuse a traced heart to the wrong side of each 4" x 7" batik rectangle; then cut out each heart. Place a heart on each quilted rectangle, about 1" from the top edge, and fuse in place. Whipstitch around the edges using

metallic or rayon thread. Refer to "All the Stitches You'll Need" on page 14 as needed.

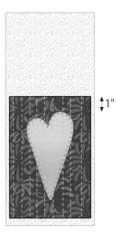

1"

3. Place a piece of rickrack across the top edge of each quilted rectangle. Baste in place, ⅛" from the edge.

4. With right sides together, place a 4½" x 5½" batik rectangle on top of each quilted rectangle, aligning the top raw edges. Sew the pieces together using a ¼"-wide seam allowance and stitching through the fabric and batting. Press the rectangles open from the front. Machine quilt the roof rectangles.

5. Trace the house pattern on page 69 onto template plastic, being sure to include the dashed line. Cut out the house, cutting directly on the solid line.

6. Lay the template on top of each house, aligning the roof placement line with the seam line as shown. Use a water-soluble marker to trace around the roof, sides, and bottom of the template. Remove the template. Using a rotary cutter and ruler, trim away the excess fabric and batting, cutting directly on the traced line.

7. Apply fusible web to the wrong side of the 4" x 6" light-value rectangle and then cut the rectangle into ¾" x 3¼" rectangles. Use the alphabet rubber stamps and black stamp pad to stamp a word of your choice on each rectangle. (I chose the words *admiration, friendship, love, adoration,* and *devotion.*) Remove the paper backing and fuse a rectangle on each heart as shown in the photo on page 64. Using a light-blue seed bead as a stop bead, sew purple sequins and beads to the corners of the rectangles with light-gray beading thread.

ASSEMBLY

1. Place the houses, side by side, on the piece of interfacing, with the bottom edges extending ⅜" beyond the bottom edge of the interfacing. Using an open-toe embroidery foot and a zigzag stitch, sew the edges of the houses together as shown. These stitches will be covered by ribbon.

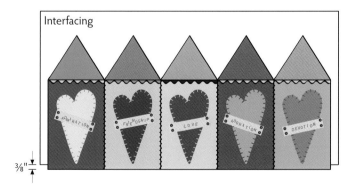

2. Place the houses and interfacing on a piece of parchment paper. Cover the houses and interfacing with another piece of parchment paper. Fuse the houses to the interfacing, being careful not to touch the sequins and beads with the hot iron.

3. Cut the blue velvet ribbon into four 7"-long pieces. Place a piece of ribbon over each zigzagged seam line. Using matching thread and a straight stitch, sew along both edges of each ribbon.

4. Place the backing rectangle on top of the houses, right sides together, with the bottom edges aligned. Using a ¼"-wide seam allowance, sew along the bottom edge *only*. Place the houses face down on the parchment paper and flip the backing fabric right side up on top of the interfacing. Fuse the backing to the interfacing.

5. On the front, baste ⅛" from the edge along all the raw edges to hold the pieces in place.

6. Use light-gray beading thread to sew eight green sequins and light-blue seed beads along each length of the velvet ribbon; use the seed bead as a stop bead.

7. Using a rotary cutter and ruler, trim the interfacing and backing even with the edges of the houses. Use sharp scissors to clip the inner points between the houses.

FINISHING AND FINAL EMBELLISHING

1. Apply fusible web to the wrong side of the 5" x 16" binding rectangle. Cut the rectangle into five 1" x 16" strips.

2. Referring to "Fusible Binding" on page 27, attach the binding to the front side, starting along the side of a house and pressing as you go. Fold the binding at the outer corners. Clip the binding at the inner points between the houses. When you reach the end of a binding strip, overlap the ends of the binding at an outer point and continue as before.

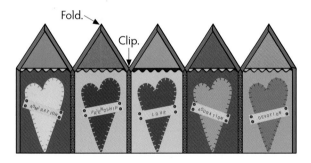

3. Use white beading thread to sew the white oval beads and gold seed beads to the edges of the rickrack; use the seed bead as a stop bead.

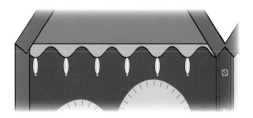

4. Refer to "Polymer-Clay Embellishments" on page 10. Using the light-blue metallic clay, make five ⅜"-diameter buttons. Use the edge of a toothpick to make indentations across the buttons and make a hole in the centers.

5. Use the purple clay to make five 1"-diameter buttons; add light-blue polka dots as described on page 11. Make a hole in the center for attaching the button.

6. On the peak of each roof, attach a purple polka-dot button and a purple sequin with a light blue seed bead; use light-gray beading thread.

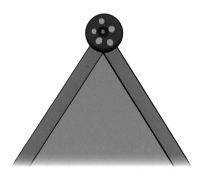

7. Use light-gray beading thread and a gold seed bead to attach a blue button to the valley between houses, covering the raw edges of the binding.

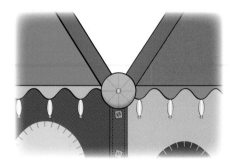

8. Cut the ribbon and decorative thread into 6"-long pieces. Wrap three or four pieces around each purple button, wrapping them once, and then tying a knot.

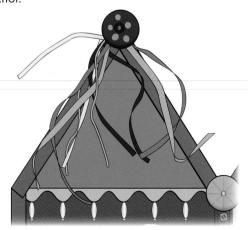

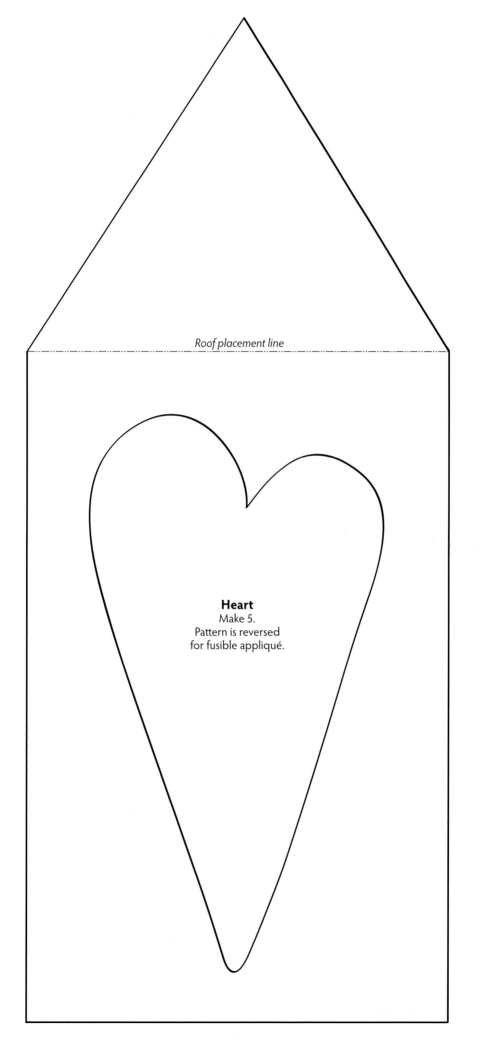

Roof placement line

Heart
Make 5.
Pattern is reversed
for fusible appliqué.

You'll have lots of fun creating these quick and easy embellished beauties using plastic shrink film. Wouldn't it be a conversation starter to *wear* a photo of your loved ones instead of leaving the photo at home on your coffee table? You can also use a favorite image or pretty embellishment in the center. A few hours are all you need to make one of these.

◀ Finished size: 2½" x 2½", excluding dangling beads

WHAT YOU'LL NEED
materials

1 rectangle, 3" x 6", of blue felt*

1 rectangle, 2" x 3", of orange-batik fabric

1 rectangle, 2" x 3", of paper-backed fusible web

1 rectangle, 2" x 3", of heavyweight, double-sided fusible interfacing

*You may need a larger piece of felt, depending on which adornment you make.

embellishments

1 image (use a favorite photo or an image on page 73)

Inkjet-printable shrink film

3 brass charms, ½" diameter

3 orange beads, size 6/0

3 white pearl-like beads, size 4 mm

3 orange seed beads, size 11/0

Pink rayon thread

Orange rayon thread

Blue rayon floss

Beading thread

tools and supplies

Freezer paper

Hand towel

⅛" hole punch

Parchment paper

Pin back, 1" long (optional)

Ribbon necklace (optional)

Rotary cutter with a pinking blade

Spray can of clear acrylic sealer, matte finish

embellishing tips

You can use up bits and pieces of the shrink film by adhering them to an 8½" x 11" piece of paper, and then resending the paper through the printer.

ASSEMBLY

1. Start with a 2" x 3" image of your choice. Print the image onto shrink film following the manufacturer's instructions. Use a rotary cutter and ruler to cut out the image. Then punch holes along the edges using the ⅛" hole punch.

2. Place the film in a conventional oven or toaster oven on a piece of parchment paper; follow the manufacturer's directions to shrink the film. (The film will first curl up, and then flatten out as it shrinks.) After the film has cooled, spray it with acrylic sealer.

3. Choose the shape for the adornment from the patterns on page 74. Trace the chosen shape twice onto the dull side of the freezer paper. Iron the shiny side of the freezer paper to the piece of blue felt. Cut out the shapes, cutting directly on the line.

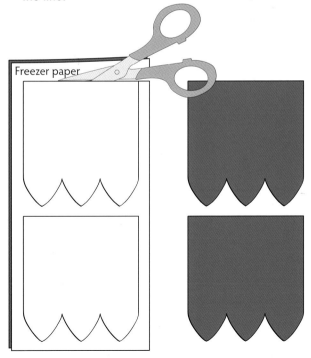

Freezer paper

4. Apply fusible web to the wrong side of the orange-batik rectangle. Using a rotary cutter with a pinking blade, trim the batik rectangle so that it's ¼" larger than the shrink-film embellishment on all sides. Remove the shrink-film embellishment. Center and fuse the trimmed rectangle to one felt shape.

5. Using blue rayon floss, stitch French knots around the edges of the fused rectangle. Refer to "All the Stitches You'll Need" on page 14 as needed. Center the shrink-film embellishment on the rectangle and whipstitch in place with pink thread.

6. Use orange thread to stitch the three brass charms onto the felt.

7. Cut a piece of interfacing ¼" smaller than the felt on all sides. Place the felt piece, embellished side down, on the hand towel. Place the interfacing on the felt, cover with parchment paper, and press with a hot, dry iron.

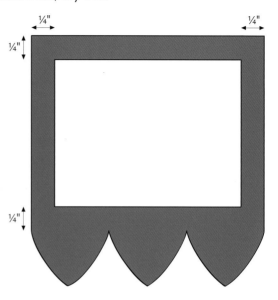

8. If you're making a pin, sew the pin back to the second felt shape.

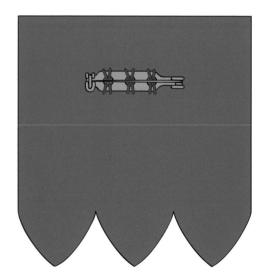

9. Place the wrong side of the second felt shape on top of the interfacing with the edges of the felt pieces aligned. Press to fuse, try to avoid pressing on top of the pin. Whipstitch around the entire piece using orange thread.

10. Create a trio of beads with the orange beads and white pearl-like beads; use the orange seed bead as a stop bead. Make three. Add the beads to the bottom edge as shown using beading thread.

11. If the adornment is going to be a necklace, attach a ribbon to the top. Lay the ribbon along the edge and whipstitch over the ribbon using a matching thread color.

Print full-size onto shrink film.

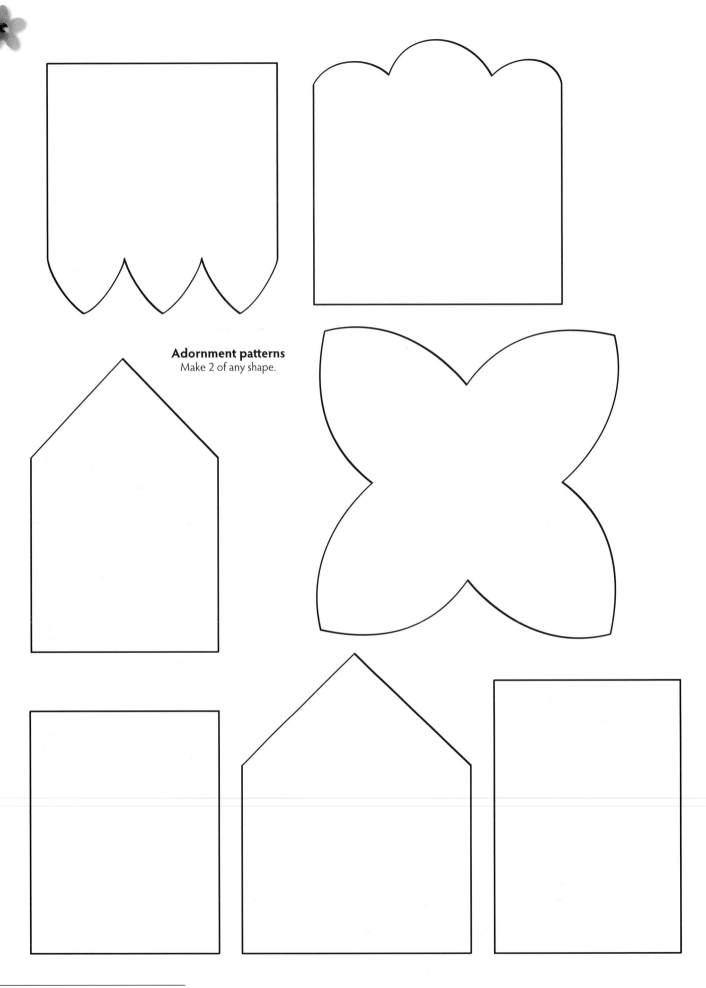

Adornment patterns
Make 2 of any shape.

inspiration GALLERY

I put my heart into every piece I create. These quilts and fiber-art pieces show how you can combine multiple techniques and multiple projects to create amazing mementos. As you'll see in the photo captions, not all of your embellished projects need to be as small as the projects in this book.

Motherhood, 28" x 31"

Family Musings in Blue, 32½" x 37"

Ride On (open), 10" x 60"

Ride On (closed), 10" x 10½"

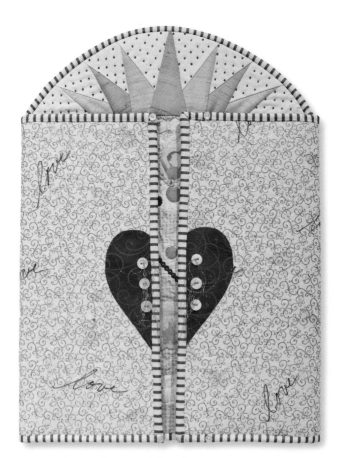

Time After Time (closed), 15½" x 21½"

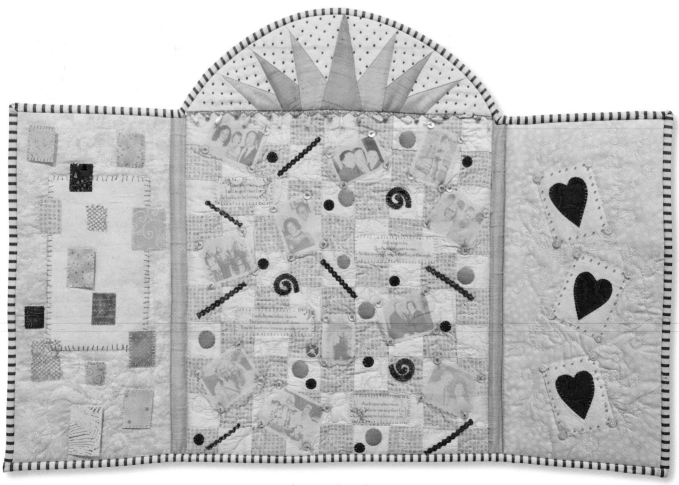

Time After Time (open), 31" x 21½"

A Shrine for Planet Earth, 47" x 57"

RESOURCES

Many of the supplies listed below can be found at your local quilt, bead, or craft shop. If you can't find them locally, try these websites.

Beads

Fire Mountain Gems and Beads
www.firemountaingems.com

Shipwreck Beads
www.shipwreckbeads.com

Brass Charms

Fancifuls Inc.
www.fancifulsinc.com

Inkjet-Printable Shrink Film

Grafix
www.grafixarts.com

Peltex II Interfacing

Jo-Ann Fabric and Craft Stores
www.joann.com

Printable Fabric Sheets

The Electric Quilt Company
www.electricquilt.com

June Tailor Inc.
www.junetailor.com

Printed Treasures
www.printedtreasures.com

about the AUTHOR

Cheryl Lynch made her first quilt out of Marimekko fabric as an impoverished chemistry graduate student at the Massachusetts Institute of Technology. Another 17 years would pass before she completed her second quilt—after a corporate career and child rearing.

When she moved to Pennsylvania in 1992, both her sons were in school. She started taking quilting classes at the local quilt shops, and it didn't take long before she fell in love with everything about quilting and started to design her own quilts. Cheryl then started teaching at a local quilt shop and published her own Judaic pattern line.

Cheryl's love of color and texture led her to add beads, buttons, and charms to her quilts. Soon she was adding all different kinds of mementos to her creations. Her quilts have been published in national quilt magazines and won ribbons in quilt shows and museums. Her first book, ¡Quilt Fiesta! (Martingale, 2011), created quite a buzz about designing quilts from ceramic Mexican tiles. It was featured on The Quilt Show with Alex Anderson and Ricky Tims.

Cheryl lives near Philadelphia with her husband, Don, and her empty-nest dog, Bailey. Her grown sons live nearby. She loves to travel and roam the aisles of hardware stores for design inspiration. To see more of Cheryl's work, visit her website at www.cheryllynchquilts.com or her blog at www.cheryllynchquilts.blogspot.com.

2 1982 03025 9836